AMONG MAYA RUINS

by LONNIE PELLETIER

COPYRIGHT INFORMATION

Copyright@2017 by Lonnie Pelletier

All rights reserved. No part of this book may be reproduced, or transmitted by any means, without the prior written permission of the publisher, except in the case of a reviewer, who may quote brief passages. In the case of photocopying or other reprographic copying, users must obtain a license from the author or Access Copyright.

Cover design by Lonnie P. Pelletier
Editing by Martha Todd
Photography by
      Martha Todd and
      Lonnie Pelletier
Instar Publishing Ltd.

Pelletier, Lonnie, 1943, author
Among Maya Ruins / Lonnie Paul Pelletier
ISBN 978-1-928151-12-8

Subjects:
1. Maya historical ruins
2. Archaeology
3. Architectural summary
4. Travel in Mexico

AMONG MAYA RUINS

By Lonnie Pelletier

OTHER BOOKS BY LONNIE PELLETIER:

100 Travel Moments In 42 Countries
Exoplanets - 101 Spacescapes
Galaxies - 65 Exoplanet Worlds
Galaxies For Kids
More Galaxies For Kids
Memory Search
Pelletier Chronicles - 500 Years
Art Quest
Sea Scout Sea
Life's Third Quarter
Gulf Island Suite
Prairie Nostalgia

CONTENTS

	page
COPYRIGHT PAGE	2
MAYA RUINS INDEX	6
THE MAP OF THE RUINS	7
CAVES AND CENOTES	8
LARGER MUSEUMS	8
NOTES REGARDING SPELLING	8
FORWARD	9
A YUCATAN JOURNEY	15
IDEAL TOUR ROUTES	139
RECOMMENDED HOTELS	143
ENJOYABLE BOOKS ON MAYA CULTURE	146
MAYA RUINS ALPHABETICALLY	149

***

MAYA RUINS INDEX

	page
1. Mayapan	19
2. Xkambo (X'Cambo)	21
3. Dzibilchaltun	22
4. Oxkintok	31
5. Ake	35
6. Edzna	42
7. Ek Balam	52
8. Chichen Itza	55
9. Tulum	75
10. Coba	78
11. Labna	91
12. Xlapac	93
13. Sayil	94
14. Kabah	96
15. Uxmal	98
16. Balamku	107
17. Calakmul	110
18. Chicanna	117
19. Xpujil	119
20. Becan	121
21. Dzibanche	123
22. Kinichna	125

The map shows our base location in Uaymitun and the cities of our visits. Ruins are numbered in order of visiting.

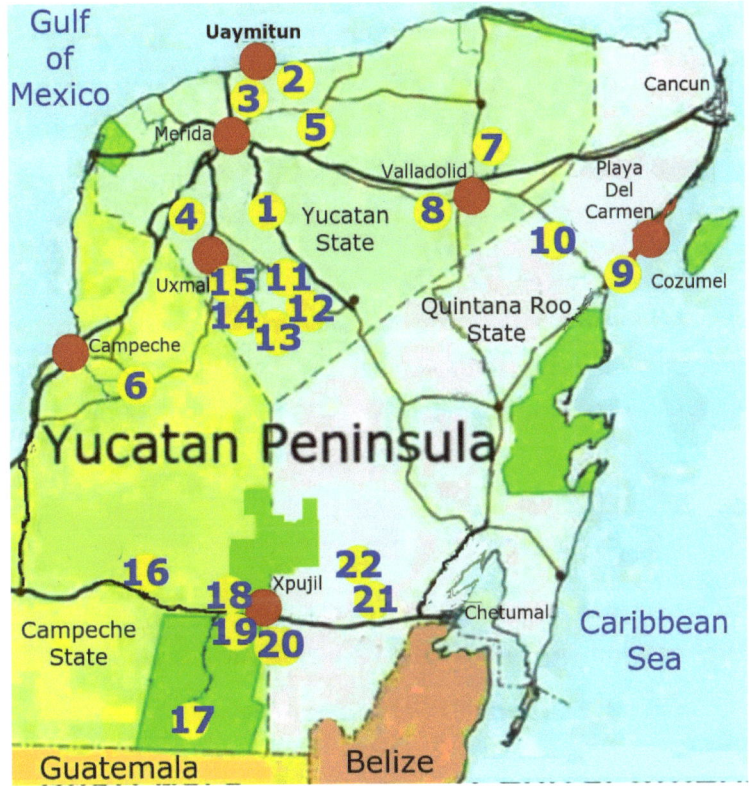

CAVES AND CENOTES

	page
Gruta Balankanche	61
Palomitas Cenote	64
Grutas de Loltun	90

LARGER MUSEUMS

	page
Museum of the Maya People, Dzibilchaltun	25
El Gran Museo del Mundo Maya, Mérida	33
San Miguel Fort Archaeological Museum	41
El Palacio Municipal, Valladolid	50
Regional Museum of Anthropology, Mérida	83

NOTES REGARDING SPELLING

When writing in Spanish the names of the cities, caves and cenotes require accents on the last syllable. In English it is unnecessary to accent Mayan words as though writing in Spanish.

I also chose to use Canadian spelling. The difference is not major and most often is that of colour (not being color), favourite (not being favorite), centre (not being center) *and so on*.

The word *Maya* as a noun and an adjective describes the people and their culture. The word *Mayan* is used correctly in referring to the language of the Maya, which includes Mayan hieroglyphs.

FORWARD

The field of Maya archaeology is in a state of flux as interpretations of complex social, economic, political and religious organizations of the Maya World seems to change consistently. Generations of archaeologists have labored to make sense of the many mysteries and contradictions. For that and the practical reason that I am not an archeologist, my writing is more of *a guide to the beauty and enjoyment of Maya architecture.*

I have enjoyed imagining mysterious cities hidden in the jungle as lost civilizations. The reality was that I was now driving a new car and could only romanticize with a lack of road signs and massive pot-holes.

The predecessors of the Maya lived on the Peninsula for thousands of years before living in structured settlements. The National Institute of Anthropology (INAH - Mexico) states that over 1600 archaeological zones may now be explored, all presenting exciting designs of ancient architecture and community planning. It is INAH that is responsible for the administration and management of these sites.

In the mid-eighteen hundreds, Maya civilization was still being represented by adventurers, explorers and writers, who sought fame and fortune by spinning incredible stories. Serious studies only began after the 1870's. Finally in the 1940's archaeologists changed from a mentality of looking for great temples and pyramids to the inclusion of studying the life of the masses.

Attempts to decipher the ancient scripts had already begun, but only in 1960 was the *code of glyphs*, characters of Mayan writing, broken. Tourism as a major industry only began in 1971 on the Yucatan Peninsula.

In order to enjoy Maya culture the periods may relate to:
1. *Olmec* artifacts and colossal stone heads were primarily from 1200 BC to 400 BC. They overlapped Maya culture in some of the same areas, but by 600 BC the *Maya* had surpassed the Olmec in the size of centres and architectural development.
2. *Preclassic Period of the Maya* from pottery found from as early as 2000 BC.
3. *Early Classic Period* (250 AD - 600 AD).
4. *Late Classic Period* (600 AD - 830 AD).
5. *Terminal Classic Period* (830 AD - 950 AD).
6. *Postclassic Period* (950 AD - 1400 AD).

These periods and their sub-periods often overlapped in geographical areas with different groups and styles. Ambiguity also exists when comparing dates between the archaeology and anthropology communities, with *Postclassic* often stated as 1150 AD to 1550 AD in the latter.

Primary styles influencing Maya architecture can be stated simply. But in visiting the ruins they become obvious upon viewing.

Focusing on the three styles of Chenes, Puuc and Rio Bec will usually suffice.

Chenes Architecture, created large entries with animal and deity forms which were deemed to be an entrance to the spiritual world. Entry was often over the threshold of the creature's extended tongue. The sculpted images are usually crude and not detailed. The influence of *Chenes* architecture is throughout the Yucatan Peninsula, alongside both *Rio Bec* and *Puuc* architecture, however, it is most common n the southern area of the Yucatan Peninsula. Carved facades on both the upper and lower areas were commonly one story high, taking the shape of spirals and distorted beings. *Chenes* structures didn't use columns, glyphic inscriptions or stelaes as did the other two styles.

Rio Bec is characterized by emphasising the vertical using both false towers and rooms with slender pyramids. The southern route across the Yucatan Peninsula, near the Guatemalan border, forms the centre of this style. The styles all achieved the same symbolic purpose - to represent a sacred cave. But they used different methods to symbolise this sacred place of creation. The *Rio Bec* style is often a combination of styles that includes *Chenes,* in that false doors and steps too steep to be used, are common.

Puuc has an emphasis on *art in architecture*. Geometrical design is paramount, with the beautiful city of Uxmal being the beginning of the *Puuc Route* of splendid architecture. Complicated, elaborate and detailed design work were a part of the structures. A stone fretwork was often used to create an image of an *Underworld God or Monster*. That is, there is no tablet or single stone representing an entire subject. Each stone itself is an unmeaning fractional portion within a theme.

The issue of exceptions and overlapping styles is so common that enjoying visual moments far supersedes any recommendation to ascertain specific definition of styles. By the time the Spanish arrived in the 1500's, the Yucatan was divided into nineteen provinces, with a multitude of leaders and numerous hierarchies. For an easier enjoyment of reading, I will not attempt to describe the hundreds of liaisons and wars.

Many religious traditions co-existed with a range of gods, most with multiple manifestations. The meaning of these gods constantly doubled or changed aspect, or were superimposed on one another. Aside from a brief summary of the gods of the Maya World, I will leave the challenge of that ongoing interpretation of over two hundred gods, each beautifully portrayed in sculpture and bas-reliefs - to others.

A very short list follows, *with just enough information to aid in enjoying the ruins*.

1. *Chaac* was important as the god of rain, also known as God B. Due to his importance, human sacrifices were often dedicated to him.
2. *Ah Puch*, (also *Kisin, Ah Kin*, or *God A*. shown in skeletal form) was the god of death.
3. *Huapu* was one of the twins representing the planet Venus.
4. *Xbalanque* was the other twin.
5. Their ancestor was *Yax Balam* (or the *Green Monster*) the symbol of the sun.
6. *Itzam Cab Ain* was the Earth Monster in the form of an iguana or alligator.
7. *Itzamna* the father of the gods, who created the world.
8. *Ixchel* was his wife, goddess of the moon, later becoming the goddess of maternity.
9. *K'awh* was also called *Bolon Dz'acab, Hun Racan* and God K. He was associated with blood and royal sperm, distinguished by a long nose and legs in the shape of snakes.
10. *Kinich Ahau* was god of the sun.
11. *Kukulcan* was also *Quetzalcaotl* or the Feathered Serpent. He was often stated as the god of wind and of the planet Venus - in a never ending shift of *who's who* in the god world of the Maya.

I think this simple approach to the enjoyment of the sculptured gods, integrated with architecture, is more important - as over two hundred gods would be a lot of memorization - and a lot less fun.

I did climb, as most others did, all of the pyramids where access was allowable. I'm guessing that it's an instinct in all of us, as it allows us to take ownership of the pyramid, as an historic symbol. It creates the reality of *we were there*.

Like many readers, I have been frustrated by the inconsistencies found in guide books, mostly existing because the writer had never visited the subject sites. *I have only written about the sites that I have trounced upon, stumbled at, climbed, admired, or otherwise physically known.*

This then is my journey *Among Maya Ruins*.

* * *

A YUCATAN JOURNEY

The journey began in 1974. By coincidence the ruins of Chichen Itza and Uxmal coincided with a trip to view the *Atlantic Ocean*. Thanks to our guide for the three days, we stood at the pier in Progreso and viewed the Gulf of Mexico to our left, the Caribbean Ocean to our right and the Atlantic Ocean straight ahead. In actual fact, with no thanks to our guide, we had viewed the Yucatan Strait and the Gulf of Mexico. (The Atlantic is on the other side of Cuba.) It was fun though to think that we had seen the Atlantic and the Caribbean Sea at the same time from this magical peninsula.

Returning to Mexico over forty-some years of sporadic visits, my knowledge of geography improved. We were now living on the Yucatan and the waterway is also known as the Gulf Stream. More importantly, this is my account of Maya Architectural History viewed at the pace of retirement.

***

FIRST WEEK:

I had made a first-world decision. My emails to my adult children needed to include stated subjects. I initially capitalized *LIFE IS A BEACH #1* and consistently numbered my emails. As we were going to be on the Yucatan Peninsula for five months, coupled with living on the beach in a contemporary cabin, it seemed logical and a bit humorous.

Now *older* and while thinking of myself as about 53, my adult son and daughter probably think of me as *somewhere in between*. This was my alternative to an old-age-home and my lifestyle was really *life is a beach*. Martha, my constant companion *Among Maya Ruins*, is shown relaxing between tours, in our idyllic setting.

* * *

Our house is less than two hundred feet to high tide. Not a point of great philosophy, but a wonderful contemplation is my enjoyment of pelicans. One family has a nest close to us and their fishing is done directly in front. I enjoy how they go *splat*. My first enjoyment of them was with observing of how they fly rapidly about a foot off the sand and water. My second was their fishing method.

Their wings are above their bodies and I can only compare them to a large airplane of a bomber style - ill proportioned. Upon viewing a fish, they quickly fly up to about forty feet and then dive. My amusement is due to their entry into the water. Every other bird that I've viewed, dives with an elegance, a streamlined entry. The pelican goes *splat*. Within a nano second it brings its head out of the water and sits upright while digesting its meal. As I sit here writing, another two just went *splat*. I'm smiling. I wonder if they will cease to amuse me.

***

SECOND WEEK:

I have to qualify visits to Costco and Walmart in Merida as a part of enjoying Mexico. Although when I got lost driving I was saved by a tour of the colonial section of Merida and a few side journeys through new subdivisions. Living on the Gulf of Mexico, at the northern tip of the peninsula, we also explored the small towns of Highway #27, from Dzilam de Bravo on the east to Chuburna' on the west.

We were always comparing our life at Uaymitun, where we had the five month lease - and concluded that we best fit here in what are known as *beach houses*. These are some of the most unique architecturally designed and contemporary homes in the world (by my humble estimation).

However, many are *tired*, in need of refurbishing. Most are vacant twenty-plus year old homes and many show the rath of being in close proximity to the sea. The rental and for-sale photos online were usually taken when the homes were new. The concrete walls are now stained, electrical connections are rusted or in need of repair, and some of the plumbing is usually broken. It is normal to assure others that we are living in our *dream house by the ocean,* ignoring reality.

***

THIRD WEEK:

1 MAYAPAN, Yucatan

Our choice for the first of many visits to Maya ruins was one of the newer sites, that of Mayapan. It was a one and one-half hours drive away, using a ring-road around Merida. At the time we were only two of five visitors to this site. As is true of most of the archaeological sites, a bus stop is available on the highway near-by.

One-fifth of the morning's visitors arrived and left by bus. We were tempted to offer him a ride, but that would not be prudent in Mexico.

Mayapan, the capital of the Yucatan until 1450 AD, is of the Late Post-Classic period and is famous for having been the last great Maya ceremonial center. A recently discovered warrior modeled in stucco was a highlight. The stucco bas-relief is under a protecting roof and easily photographed. My initial reaction to this ruined city was like all of the sites that followed. We want to share our many photos. But I consistently reminded myself that other books with that specific purpose are superior. In my case, one or two photos per ruined city *should do it*.

Mayapan is often presented as a smaller version of Chichen Itza as in the similarity of design above. Because of that smaller size it is more manageable and enjoyable in imagining city patterns, shops, residences, walkways and even roads, those years long ago. Easily seeing the panorama of this city, while not being hurried, allowed an understanding of the city having been alive and vibrant.

The main structures on this site are:
- The Kukulcan Pyramid,
- El Caracol or the Observatory,
- The Temple of the Niches and
- The Palace.

We could also see many of the more than four thousand pyramid shaped mounds that have yet to be explored within this walled city, giving a realization of the massive undertaking of the world of archaeology.

2 X'CAMBO, Yucatan

X'Cambo, also spelled Xkambo, was chosen as a visit due to its proximity - less that twenty kilometres (12.5 miles) from our beach home. Only a small port town in its past, sites of this type are equal for being enjoyable. It had been a trading centre for salt and handicrafts to other Maya cities as far away as Campeche, Tabasco and in what are now the countries of Guatemala and Belize.

The photo also shows a typical Maya hut, the common building style of local homes beside the roads when I had last visited. Being ten kilometres away *as the pelican flies*, it made us feel like we were living among Maya ruins.

Our drive there and back was punctuated with views of groups of flamingoes parading in shallow waters in a long lagoon, on the *other side* of the highway from our house. We have not yet tired of their beautiful movements while walking in unison and in a ballet of symphony.

3 DZIBILCHALTUN, Yucatan

Dzibilchaltun was also less than one hour's drive with rural paved roads and almost no traffic. This was during Christmas week and we expected much local traffic from Merida. To our surprise, the throngs of locals were superseded by cruise ship tour groups. The nearby town of Progreso was now hosting as many as two cruise ships per day. Forty-two years had past since my last visit to this specific Maya ruin.

Thanks to the same guide that gave us a taxi lift to Progreso so many years ago, we had visited Dzibilchaltun on the way from Merida. Our driver, at that time, had insisted that I walk the ceremonial walk-way to the main building. The path is called a *Sacbe*. I remember being intrigued by the fact that this was a long, straight and narrow path, with dense overhanging jungle branches. He had explained that this walk-way was used for processions with a full regatta of colorful head dresses and robes, *strange and fanciful as the ornamentation on their buildings,* one-thousand years prior.

The sixteen square kilometres of Dzibilchaltun are now known as one of the longest inhabited of ancient Maya cities with occupation beginning in 500 BC. From the Temple of the Seven Dolls the sculpted dolls had already been removed and saved in the national museum in 1974. The inscriptions that I viewed on its interior walls then, were related to its history. Only later, in 1998, was the importance of this site established and other structures uncovered and given their due presentation.

Only in this, my second visit, was anyone aware of the importance of Dzibilchaltun as a huge settlement of eight thousand known structures. In 1974, I had walked up a rural path with no one else around - to what I initially perceived, from a distance, as being a stone hut, built on a rock pedestal. We now know that the *hut*, the *Temple of the Seven Dolls*, was built prior to 800 AD. The jungle is removed and the pathway is now widened with rock shoulders.

The ancient graffiti, that I had viewed painted on the interior rocks is now displayed in the site's museum and I had been able to view it within its original setting. Public entrance to the Temple is no longer allowed.
A large plaza accompanies a palace with more than one-hundred rooms - at the opposite end of the *Sacbe* near the *Xlacah cenote*. Like some of the other Maya sites, there is a Spanish chapel centered in the plaza, built later in the fifteen hundreds - proclaiming the superiority of the conquering religion.

When I was a younger man, our driver had said that I was able to view a site that not everyone visited or even knew of. I had let my imagination soar then. As I walked the total distance of the ceremonial Sacbe, I had felt I was exploring in the true archaeological sense.

Forty-two years later in 2016 and 2017, and finding that the essence of the site was only discovered in 1998 - I celebrated and bought a tourist coffee mug with the Temple of the Seven Dolls on it. There is something relevant to viewing a one-thousand year old site in that manner - at intervals of almost one-half century. In the future, I hope to look at my Dzibilchaltun coffee mug and try to understand what that relevance is.

The main structures on this site are:
- The Temple of the Seven Dolls,
- The Central Plaza,
- The South Plaza,
- The structures with Monoliths and
- The clusters of residential foundations,

The reality of residences is easier to imagine at this site. Once the perishable material of the roof and walls is understood, the homes and their layouts are very real. The clusters are marked for easy viewing.

***

The Museum of the Maya People on the Dzibilchaltun site is superb and was wonderful to stroll through in conjunction to this site and others. It became obvious with this visit that the Maya possessed all of the minor arts, which coexisted with architecture, but only imperishable stone survived. The vase is one exception.

The separate farm house structures at the back of the museum beautifully shows the advancement of the standard of living on the peninsula within the last forty years. I would later discover that those changes were not consistent.

***

FOURTH WEEK:

We now waited for the Christmas break to be over before touring further south of Merida. The northern part of the Yucatan map is punctuated with names of villages, and we expected town centres as we had viewed and enjoyed in central Mexico. The towns were originally built around a centre square, built in front of a large church, however economic systems had changed and Mexican culture had changed.

As in most parts of the world, the largest city within an hour's drive was a draw for the youth. The towns here are now too close to be valid as a stand-alone community. We made the observation that youth is both motorized and armed with cell phones with internet influencing communication. Many had moved on.

In visiting Celestun, to the west, we found out how bad the state highways could be. The pavement was good, but the potholes were not. They could have qualified as sink-holes. This is not a criticism of the highways department maintenance crews, but rather a fault of the road crossing marshes and lagoons. They would have been impossible to maintain. But we made it!
Celestun youth, that is the ones that stayed at home, sell small boat tours to tourists primarily from cruise ships. Their clientele pays enormous dollars, usually actual American dollars, for one hour of possibly seeing flamingoes. As someone living on the north coast peninsula, we were able to view flamingoes in small or

even large flocks, on *our* lagoon, on any given day. In driving around many of the streets, some marked, some gravel or washed away, we understood that we were seeing a lack of economic development and a lack of opportunity related to employment for anyone living there.

That overview was consistent for us in all of the Highway #27 communities. Our *Plan B* for a retirement village was Ajijic on Lake Chapala. These areas did not compare to that particular *sense of community*. We visited the villages from Chuburna on the west to Dzilam de Bravo on the east. Something had happened to this beautiful coast and it probably would not be anyone's *Plan A* for retirement.

The entire area was framed with a beautiful beach. Many of the beach homes were architectural wonders. Their photographs may be viewed on the *Progreso Vacations*, or *Yucatan Vacations* web site. Beach homes were now vacant with less than ten percent being occupied. We pondered the question of what had happened. We hoped that five months living in the area would allow us an understanding.

***

FIFTH WEEK:

Insurance is the bulk of the cost of renting a vehicle in Mexico, with the cost of the car rental being one-fifth of the total. It was obvious that we should be able to get a long-term price break, as compared to the daily rate multiplied. All of the larger rental firms refused any rental longer than one-month, with the proviso that the car be returned for a new contract each thirty days.

After one month we switched to *Yucatan Vacation*s. The saving was over twenty-five percent. The car photo is at the back of our cabin. We had decided that the Gulf of Mexico was our front yard with the highway at the back.

I had developed confidence in maintaining a Mexican house. We picked up our drinking water from one of the stores supplying it and could do it easily without much thought. Our garbage was easy as we dropped off a large black bag each time we went for water. Gas for cooking was now coordinated with a supplier who agreed to honk his truck horn every few weeks when going by.

This was as normal as buying fish, prawns, crab and even lobster from our supplier, Roberto. His dilapidated car seemed to make it by every other week. His price was probably higher than the local market, but the quality of his product was wonderfully fresh and perfect.

Internet connection was solved easily by using a plan from *Telmex* that allowed our newly purchased Mexican cell phone to have almost unlimited access to the web. Whenever needed we set the cell phone to be our *hot spot* and tethered our computers and eBook Readers to the cell phone via the data plan. No *brick and mortar* home plan was needed.

The proviso is that a Mexican cell phone needed to be purchased, however some of the best phones were under 1000 pesos. That even included the first month of data. The cost of ongoing data and phone service worked out to 10 pesos per day. I concluded that in the future, in other regions of Mexico, this would be a perfect data system. A system that could have been complex or costly, now seemed easy and inexpensive.

In conjunction to this, my operating system is with a chromebook. Last year in Bali and Borneo and the year before that in Costa Rica, a public mannerism was obvious. Due to having important and necessarily secure data, each individual protected their laptops *with their life.* When sitting on the beach, or while canoeing in the jungle, they carried their laptops. There is a better system, as having all of my data in the *clouds of google* and other services, I therefore have no information in my laptop that is relevant. Should my laptop be stolen from *my room*, I will lose a very small amount as dollar value, and be confronted with inconvenience only.

A further note is that *cloud drive* is accessible on our cell phone in our car. Google Maps also worked well when searching hotel address - but not so well in giving directions for Maya ruins. Our *Apps* include a flashlight, weather, peso conversion, local news and even an anti-mosquito sound (which actually works) - hardly eighteen century exploring.

We now had a maid and pool vacuuming service and due to sand blowing from our beach - we scheduled them for each second Thursday. Our original option of needing to have rented a condo for such packaged services now seemed remote. We were relaxed instead, in a single-family home and *life was a beach*.

* * *

SIXTH WEEK:

4 OXKINTOK, Yucatan

Logically we would view the ruins nearest us first and we chose Oxkintok. It was only a two hour drive, but the three kilometre road off the paved highway was a surprise. Only lightly graveled and one way, it would have been a challenge in the rain. A second priority for visiting this site was the architecture and town planning of this ancient city that we had read about. Being our first site with rolling hills and large plazas, it seemed to be alive. In this setting, we could easily imagine the ancient Maya in their market square with the hustle and bustle of a few thousand individuals in specifically defined activities.

The buildings were different than we had seen due to *Puuc influence* and showed us the Classic Period of AD 400 to 700. The *Zona Puuc* includes the sites of Uxmal, Kabah, Labna, Xlapak and Sayil. For us the *Puuc Era* meant that we were to view Greek-like pillar patterns in the outer walls of the buildings, with designs of geometric shapes. This is not a complex design concept to appreciate, as in visiting many ruins it is easy to recognize this stylized difference when comparing.

Here it was the decorative patterns of the imitation pillars, carved approximately 1500 years ago, as decoration on the walls, that intrigued us.

This Maya site was usual in that a minimum of a five hour visit seemed necessary to enjoy the ambiance and our personal imagination of historic happenings. As in X'Cambo, no modern facilities existed except for wash rooms. On this day in January, only one other visiting group of four showed up and we found that they lived in the local area. A larger more accessible road was probably not needed, but we felt sorry for the many tourists who missed out in not viewing this ruined city.

One mid-sized pyramid is noted for its Labyrinth, which contains a dark maze on three levels with an accessible entrance. The entrance was known to be to the *Underworld of the Gods* that only the Lord of Oxkintok could use. We didn't crawl in far as we were more interested in a group of writings. One of the three structure complexes had contained inscriptions. We found that they were no longer on the site as we had thought, but two days later we viewed those inscriptions, at *El Gran Museo Del Mundo Maya*, in Merida.

There are three structure complexes on this large site:
- *Dzib*, which contains the Labyrinth,
- *May*, which contains two Pyramids and a raised residential compound, and
- The *Ah Canul* complex with two large buildings, one with a detailed facade.

* * *

El Gran Museo del Mundo Maya in Merida was as it promised, a presentation of t*he ancient and modern, traditional and changeable, unique and diverse - of one of the largest civilizations of the human race*. The architecture of the museum building was also enjoyable to appreciate and utilize.

Ancient Mexican manuscript books called codices, are comprised of painted pictographs, ideograms and phonetic symbols. Reproductions of these works, the originals being in Europe and the USA, are on display here. These are the type of works that the Spanish missionaries destroyed due to their belief that they were blasphemous. They are different than hieroglyphs in that they are in manuscript form, not as a carving.

We later found that three other *world-class* archaeological Yucatan Peninsula museums and they would also help in our understanding of the Maya World. They were the *Regional Museum of Anthropology* in Merida, *Museum of the Maya People*, in Dzibilchaltun and the *San Gabriel Fort Museum* on the outskirts of Campeche.

***

SEVENTH WEEK:

5 AKE, Yucatan

Ake was a site that should have been a quick one hour drive from our home base in Uaymitun. It seemed to be clearly marked on our tourist map and the drive should take us past henequen fields and through three small towns. However roads signs to it were not to be. We zig-zagged through the countryside and did find it with the help of three locals. I initially wondered how anyone could do our site tours without a basic knowledge of Spanish and I finally concluded at this point that conversational Spanish was very much needed. We were far from the tourist world of *all inclusive hotels*.

In finding the town abutting Ake, past El Muele, one of three towns not on any of my road maps, one sign existed. It was a directional arrow, one kilometre from the site. We were surprised to finally find even this arrow. Many times on the roads of Mexico, I would stay on the best of two choices in roads, only judging by the wear in the asphalt, and if I chose correctly would end up at the destination. This was the case.

Ake is noted for two issues, both ongoing questions by archaeologists. The buildings, from as early as 300 AD, all have curved corners. The second was the thirty-five columns on an elevated building platform, the *Edifice of the Pilasters*. Like many statements found in either books on the subject or in tourist brochures, words do not define the visual dynamic.

Seeing the effect of massive columns viewed from below on the large plaza area, gave the impression that this structure with its massive roof, would have made the desired statement of awe and of pride among its people. The roof had been made of perishable material, however the columns were not. Like every stepping stone here, the column stones were huge, each at least one cubic metre (cubic yard) in size. Much smaller stones of only a few centimetres/inches were used for decorative effect.

The realization is that each Maya site is unique. These were individual cities with an inspired personality. Ake was the least *manicured* that we had seen. The huge building stones were crude and rustic and seemed to be just as years of rain and wind would have left them - over eighteen-hundred years. The structures were the most primitive that we had seen, an evocation for a day that seemed to be one of exploration and discovery.

Like other ruins that are not included in what seems to be a standard list for viewing, we enjoyed our experience without the babel of guides, opinionated tourists and aggressive hawkers. One lone ticket seller opened the wash room for us and a group of three individuals (from

Belgium) were leaving when we arrived.

A well known tourist guidebook suggested that a henequen (sisal) manufacturing plant was *nearby*. That was not the case. The plant is at the gate of the Maya site. The plant was not only operational, but we were able to watch the process. Seeing the henequen in bundles, just brought from the fields - and seeing the rudimentary equipment that created the final product, was a treat.

Martha and I have lived on wheat farms where stukes were tied with binder-twine, left to dry, then harvested with a threshing machine. I remember when my grandfather pulled a binder with horses, then later by tractor. In the wheat fields of the world, *combines* then replaced *binders,* which had relied on henequen twine.

The ships of the world also replaced their massive use of the product for rope. We knew this factory was an unusually lucky find as mechanization and the invention of nylon had brought obsolescence to henequen processing. It was once a massive and main product of the Yucatan and we would later be driving past the vast and retired, non-producing henequen fields.

The original main building was now missing a roof and was past a need of repair. The equipment was over one-hundred years old. It was styled as factories were in the early eighteen-hundreds and the few walls that were standing had a large hacienda look, with arches and elaborate carving in its walls. The process where the leaves were made into twine, then twirled into blocks, had been moved from there to the low-slung building on the side, twenty-feet from the gate of Ake.

There are a number of henequen machines on display in museums in Mexico. This, though, was the real thing. If you are a bit older than young, and can remember binder-twine, I highly recommend walking about this small factory.

* * *

As we had done before, we stopped at a *Cocina*. Often called *Mi Cocina* or similar, this translates as, *My kitchen*. Each of these ladies has their personal recipes. They are not restaurants and they have a limited menu, as if stopping by someone's kitchen. The test is if there are a large number of locals. We patiently waited in-line here, in the town of Motul and had an excellent *chicken mole*.

We had dined in a number of haciendas on the peninsula and Hacienda Teya just outside of Merida, was our favourite, but paying for a *five star meal* and receiving *five star quality* is too easy. Built in 1683, Teya is apparently a choice of many with *refined tastes*, (their words, not mine) - with photos in their lobby to prove it. The Clinton family and Queen Sofia of Spain have enjoyed their ambiance. It was always a better experience to dine in local *kitchens* and relish the fine *sabors* of Mexico (tastes) - most often surprising and wonderful.

* * *

EIGHTH WEEK:

As now seemed normal, I enjoyed coconut water and coconut meat. It was from our yard and was by my perception: *home-grown*. Initially I was armed with only a sharp rusty spade (a shovel) and a kitchen knife as tools. Our landlords had not left any actual tools. The challenge was fun - in semi-retirement I had the time. By the second coconut I had a better system (the first was ridiculous).

We had booked four days in Campeche and here could see the remnants left by Drake, Morgan and other 17th century pirates, and also the ruins at Edzna. In reading about it, Campeche seemed like an exciting city of history and architecture and it did not let us down.

It was a beautiful day for travel. By our first observation, Campeche was the cleanest city in Mexico, with not a scrap of garbage to be viewed! The historical centre seemed everything a colonial walled city could be. We talked of this being like Europe in sophistication.

The sites within the city were many and our walking tours along with our guided city tour gave us an insight into five hundred years of its past. Many churches were on the tours along with the City Theatre, the State and the Municipal Archives, the House of Justice, the large Autonomous University of Campeche, the Plaza of the Fourth of October, the Gates of San Francisco, and many monuments and sculptures.

There is a handicap for a city being a *World Heritage Site*. Campeche was a modern commercial centre in the context of business. However, the offices and retail buildings, in that contemporary context, are not allowed to renovate the exteriors of their premises. Many of the staff of the companies that I observed, seemed to want to *break out* into the modern world. There is a compromise in using technology in antique surroundings. This was a personal observation that I had not noticed in other areas, where only specific buildings are designated *heritage*. Only one high-rise existed just outside of the walls and it seemed out of place. But the overview of heritage being on display was ideal for tourists and that fact flaunted the city's uniqueness in a wonderful way.

San Miguel Fort Archaeological Museum is an incredible museum. **San Gabriel Fort** had a small museum of arms and period pieces and the two fortifications were on the outskirts. But to get there, no signs seemed to be available on the main roads. The only signs were within a few feet of the forts themselves. In fact we got lost going to both. Both entrances shown on Google Maps were under construction and useless to us.

I should mention that enjoyment of being lost in searching for destinations can only be had with the proper partner. Martha is very relaxed (as I am) in going the few extra blocks or miles. Our rationalization is that we are touring in order to see the country. The extra distance gives us more views. Fortunately only a few minutes, or an hour is used up. Not very efficient, but in this case we saw a lot of Campeche that we normally would not see - including the poorer sections of town.

***

6 EDZNA, Campeche

Signs were not to be found on roads leading out of Campeche, but as was often the case we drove by (cardinal) direction alone. We finally observed that Edzna is a Maya ruin that can be described as awesome. This was a city inhabited from 600 BC to 1450 AD.

Upon entering the central plaza, I looked to my left to discover the most awe inspiring view. It was the *Great Acropolis*, 98 feet high with a base of 530 feet wide, filled with open rooms, not like any pyramid that I had ever viewed. Usually referred to as a five-floor building, the height meant something else to me.

Inner contemporary office ceilings are usually eight feet high - then add two feet for concrete floors and drop-ceilings with mechanical services. My thoughts were of each normal storey being ten feet high. One-hundred feet now makes a ten storey building. Standing at the base of this structure was like standing below and looking up at a ten storey building - with its construction starting approximately two thousand years ago!

I have referred to each Maya site being different and this great building alone gave us a reason to visit this unique world. The other buildings were important as were the beautifully carved masks and glyphs, but as tourists to the Maya World we will never forget the dynamic emotion of seeing this *Great Acropolis*. The people of its time must have been very inspired and proud of their structure.

The main structures on this site are:
- The Great Acropolis,
- The Small Acropolis,
- The Central Plaza,
- The Ball Court,
- The Platform of the Knives,
- Nohoch-na as above, and
- The South Temple.

* * *

Our choice was to return to Campeche by a different route, giving us a variety of country-side views. The way back included a toll highway. As we drove up to the toll gate something seemed amiss. One man on my right was waving me in with his hat and yelling hurry-up in Spanish. Five others were standing next to the toll both. One had his hat out asking for money. I replied that I would pay the gentleman in charge, as I could see him standing in full uniform, just inside his booth. It was then I realized that they had blocked him from coming out.

The *Hat Guy* said, "*Veinte pesos!*"

I only had a fifty peso note. I took it out and I asked for change. One of the men handed me twenty pesos back.

Not sure what was happening, I asked for another ten, stating in Spanish, "You said twenty, not thirty."

Someone handed me a couple more pesos in change, and yelled in Spanish: "go - go - go."

It was then I looked to my right and saw the placards. They had to do with corruption by the Department of Highways. One stated that the land was owned by the farmers and they were not receiving anything from the tolls. As two of the men on our right shook their fists at me, I knew I was not the right person to explain their Department of Highways system to them.

I had filled up our rental car with regular gas, but it also optionally took premium. As one of the men then manually bent the barricade gate back and I floored the car for speed out of there - I wished I had filled it with premium. We obviously could now use the extra acceleration. It had a happy ending, that is we were on our way. It could have been something else. One man had been banging on our trunk and back window. Campeche state did not seem so happy to us at this point.

A few hours later, having taken a break from our exquisite hotel, a luxury booked through Expedia with discounts, I drove to the series of seafood restaurants, situated in a row, cantilevered over the seawall. They were at the start of a very modern and lengthy Malacon. It didn't seem unusual that waiters were outside on the strip of highway entering the cluster. What happened next was to the extreme.

Each waiter began waving us into their angle parking, each in front of their restaurant. We had chosen one that was three in, that is our intention was to drive by the first two. Some of the waiters began demanding loudly that I roll down my window or turn in. I slowed the car and one stood in front of my car hood trying to stop me. I let the car slowly move forward and he moved. Others started pounding on our trunk and car roof.

One man yelled in Spanish, "Do you not want to eat?"

I yelled back in Spanish, "At this moment - NO!" Coincidently he seemed to be the waiter from the restaurant that we had chosen from the signs, but we didn't want to play this rather dangerous game.

I kept driving, they fell back and we angle-parked at about the tenth restaurant. What seemed to be a very nice lady, the waitress, was standing outside and she welcomed us. We had a delicious Campeche style and Veracruz style seafood and enjoyed it, refusing to let either of the two incidences ruin our day.

I have never been accosted in Mexico in this manner. Both incidents could have transpired into something really unfortunate as our car was physically being attacked. Both happened within three hours of each other. But when travelling we never know the other side of the story. Were we only one of two vehicles to dine at the seafood restaurants that afternoon? What did we represent in our new vehicle to the individuals with their anti-establishment takeover of the tolls on the highway?

We ate at the sidewalk cafe's on 59 avenue, just a few blocks from our Campeche hotel. It was a wonderful setting for two beautiful evenings and we will remember it. With tables set on a colonial street in view of the gated entrance to the city, blocked off from traffic - an ambiance usually only viewed in Europe.

For that and the wonderful local music and friendliness, the city can be proud. We did enjoy Campeche overall and I can say that I hope that the cities systems can be more fine-tuned for tourists in the future.

***

NINTH WEEK:

A four night stay in Valladolid would allow us to experience their annual festival. Shown as both a two week fiesta and a festival in the guide book calendars, we planned our stay around it. Two of the largest Maya ruins are less than a one hour drive from this colonial city.

As we arrived early in the afternoon, we were able to check into our hotel and walk to the main city square in time for whatever would unfold. But there were no dancers, no live music and nothing indicated any type of celebration.

A few temporary sales stalls were set up and I approached a hat vendor with the question of location. He explained that, yes the festival did exist, but not in the main square. He directed me to eight blocks away, to what we in English would call the *fair grounds.*

We set off on foot and his directions were correct. We visited the largest *county fair* that either of us had ever seen. Within the crowd of possibly thousands of farmers and ranchers from the area, we were the only non-Mexicans there. In Canada and in the country to our immediate south, we have autumn fairs. Horses, cattle, sheep and any other possible local livestock are displayed with pride. This was no different.

We did get to experience the local dancing and music on stage, included in the entry fee. Vendors were offering the usual cheap prizes for winning games in one section, others were selling ceramics and knitted goods, ferris wheels were later lit up in splendor and most things seen, touched and smelled, could have been anywhere in the world. But this was Mexico and all was just a bit noisier, wilder, or heart felt, as in the case of music and dance.

We did not slight the tourist guidebooks for calling this an annual fiesta, but we did laugh at the fact that the writers had not researched the reality.

As the evening grew darker and a few patrons grew a bit drunk, we prudently bid farewell to the excitement and took a horse and carriage back to our hotel.

My reasoning was my attempt at comedy. "Why take a cab when a white stallion and an antique carriage are available?"

It was a calm and warm evening and the ride was quite a lark. The unmistakable sound of our horses hooves echoed against the beautiful colonial buildings and the wonderful smaller side streets. We were taking the long way back to our contemporary hotel. For a brief time we were in another century. Our horse's name was *Dorado*.

El Palacio Municipal, as a museum in Valladolid, was extremely interesting and told us more about the reasons behind rebellions, resentments, and the Cast War beginning in 1847.

Coinciding with the overall theme of this museum, my bias has to do with a connotation that a number of the tourist guide brochures in this city make. It is not forget the handicraft market, in this case, held on Sunday, in Valladolid.

An emphasis is placed on advertising handicrafts. The connotation to me is condescending in that it removes the concept of post secondary education presently thriving in Mexico. In fact I have met tourists who are not aware of that high level of professionalism. The tourist malls do not include Mexican or Maya architects, engineers, surveyors, doctors, lawyers and accountants. That is, the millions of tourists are presented with erroneous information relative to a real cross-section of occupations.

My rented VW (in Mexico) and my owned Ford Fiesta automobile (left in Canada), are just a couple of examples of (other) relevant *made in Mexico* products.

Embroidery in the Yucatan is an expression of traditional culture and apparently there are one hundred thousand embroiderers. Wood carving, ceramics, basket-weaving, leather working, jewelry design, and hammock manufacturing, are all meaningful and a wonderful tradition.

My bias is that in contrast I smile with a delight, each time I drive by the *Technical Institute* in Progreso (near our beach home). Coincidently, I am a painter and a writer, but it is a choice made in semi-retirement. I include painting within the concepts of arts and crafts, because it is of the non-commercial world. A lack of a large or viable cash flow is shared within all of the arts and crafts. What I cringe against is the placement of individuals in non-commercial or non-industrial environments against their will. That is an ongoing cast system.

Such is my *rant* in favor of *Cast War philosophy* and its former reason for being. The *Palacio Municipal* also seemed to present a case against the historic class system - in that same emotional manner. It is possibly a dichotomy.

***

7 EK BALAM, Yucatan

The reason to visit Ek Balam the next day, a Maya ruin just north of town, was that we knew where it was. Our choice of roads from our beach home to Valladolid was as usual using the smaller roads, rather than the large toll roads. This was not to save the cost, but rather to view these wonderful small town plazas, their old churches and the variance in the towns themselves. However, I don't recommend these types of trips to others not from the area. The roads are not marked well and it was often incumbent on me to ask directions, obviously in Spanish. But on our way prior, we had seen the turnoff sign to Ek Balam. Returning would be easy.

The city had grown mostly between 100 and 700 AD, but around 1200 AD, Ek Balam declined in size and importance. When the Spanish arrived it was still one of the largest cities in the Yucatan. The restoration project of the Ek Balam ruined city was only begun in 2010 and is still incomplete.

The reason for viewing this site is not that the Acropolis at 115 feet is the second tallest building in the Yucatan - but that a large Maya stucco frieze on its upper floor, is one of the loveliest.

The bas-relief depicts in perfect detail a governor and ruler emerging from the jaws of a monster. On either side there are two images of *Bacab*, the god that held up the *heavenly vault*. This breathtaking sculpture is almost a stark white in contrast to the stone around it, due to being stucco. Stucco, by its nature, needs to be consistently upgraded; antiquities found in rock do not. This means that the detail of that large sculpture could be maintained over the years, probably in this state being like new. Again, as each site has its uniqueness this frieze was our focus and an ingrained memory.

The main structures on this site are:
- The Acropolis,
- The North and South Plazas,
- The Oval Palace and
- The Habitation Structure,
- The Twin Pyramids and
- The Ball Court.

We did see a six foot iguana, the largest we had ever seen - walking along the edge of the site. Iguanas on these sites are plentiful and if nothing else they provide interesting subject material for photographs. They seem to like the heated sunlit rocks. This one, being of alligator length, was wider than normal, also more like an alligator. We watched it from above for as long as it posed, than were amazed at how fast it disappeared into the underbrush.

8 CHICHEN ITZA, Yucatan

The crowd at Ek Balam was larger than any previous ones encountered and we were now sharing our experiences with groups. But it did not prepare us for the next day - at Chichen Itza.

We arrived at 9:00 am, giving us enough time to experience a large site. The guide books all made note of mid-afternoon being the busiest and we were following their advice. I had visited in 1974 and Martha had been there on a tour in the nineties. As I parked the car I noticed that the car parking lot was not especially large for a well known ruined city. I then looked over to the tour bus parking lot - huge. The lineup for tickets was palatable, but then came the surprise.

In my 1974 visit, the road that my guide/taxi driver took into the site was gravel. It literally cut through, in between the large pyramid and the observatory, and still exists as a wide walking path. The reason that I remembered that layout was that our guided tour was on the north side. The guide had suggested then that we observe the astronomical observatory, called *El Caracol*, without his assistance. Chichen Itza was a city that had reached its peak in 950 AD, with settlement verified from 435 AD. This made it a major centre relative to astronomy.

Then, as all the buildings were accessible, I had climbed the oval stairs inside the observatory on my own. At the top, I had stopped and reflected on what it must have been like to be a Maya, hundreds of years prior, observing the stars with their cultural focus on the planet Venus.

The guide had mentioned that Chichen Itza was not oriented with the compass points, as were the cities built before it (Uxmal for example). The pyramids and palaces were all designed as observatories for tracking heavenly bodies, constellations and planets. The ancient Maya are now famed for their accomplishments in astronomy, mathematics and calendrics. The structures were therefore offset in line with Mercury, Venus, Mars, Jupiter and possibly Saturn. With these thoughts then, my moments in the observatory, had been complete.

At that time I had entered the very narrow stairway inside the large Kukulcan Pyramid, also called El Castillo. Due to claustrophobia warnings only a handful of others had climbed the inside steps, up a narrow passageway to the chamber. At the top interior chamber a dim light was shining on the jaguar and its green jade eyes seemed to glow. We were limited in time within the vault and were instructed to look, turn and descend immediately. Even with only a quick viewing, I knew that it was a special treat. It may have been a jaguar throne, but to me it was a replica of a jaguar in a dense jungle setting.

The surprise now was not that none of the buildings could now be entered into. That is logical as even in 1974 I wondered how long this bonus of entry might last. The issue was that there were rows of vendors with their tables of souvenirs consistently calling out "only one dollar". It was a complete decimation of the ambiance of a historic ruin. Nowhere here was there to be a quiet contemplation of history. This was the noise, look and feeling of a large circus.

The second surprise was the number of people, now over six thousand per day as an average. The reason that the ticket lineup was not large is that the bus tours had bought their tickets in bulk. By 1:00 pm on this particular Monday, the entire grounds were solid with tourists. Some knew where they were, others may have thought that they were in Disneyland. It would seem like Disneyland (or Disneyworld).

The aerial view was taken in the late 1970's, before plazas were cleared to facilitate the large groups of visitors.

I have found no comparison to the Great Ball Court, after seeing many Maya sites. The Ball Court, as the largest in Mesoamerica is wonderfully restored. However, as is the case of most of the ruins, some of the bas-reliefs have been taken away to museums. This is for both the preservation and security of these wonderful art works. The carvings on the side walls display scenes. In one a decapitated ballplayer kneels while his neck gushes blood that metamorphoses into writhing snakes. I vividly remembered that scene for over forty years.

I vaguely remember the Temple of the Warriors and walking among many pillars that in 1974 far outnumbered the fifty or so visitors on the entire site. The columns once supported wooden beams for the roof of the structure. These were an architectural innovation that first appeared at Chichen Itza.

The pillars are now blocked off protecting them from vandalism. That, added to my former inside climb, and the unique observatory experience, meant that I could not have envisioned the forty-year change at Chichen Itza on any given day.

I concluded that because of the huge number of people at this site, the government (INAH) had decided that the vendors would be allowed to set up stalls within it. It is the only site where this is allowed to happen. The contemplation of history would be lost (anyway) because of the huge numbers of visitors, all trying to hear their guides statements, many wondering whether the only value of this Maya site was to find a unique souvenir.

In leaving we saw hundreds of people still in line, and what seemed to be over two-hundred large parked buses, each coming and going every few hours.

The impressive list of structures on this site includes:
- El Castillo or Kukulcan Pyramid,
- The Temple of Warriors,
- The Great Ball Court,

- The Observatory or El Caracol,
- The Temple of the Jaguars,
- The Temple of the Bearded Man,
- The Tzompatli,
- The Platform of Venus,
- The Platform of the Eagles,
- The Temple of the Great Tables
- The Plaza of a Thousand Columns,
- The Market,
- The Church,
- The Chichanchob,
- The Deer House,
- The Temazcal or Steam Bath,
- The Nunnery, and
- The Akab Dzib.

The most famous of all Sacred Cenotes, also called *Cenote of Sacrifice*, is here. Vendors now line both sides of the wide path from the *Castillo* to this cenote, possibly the only polluted cenote in the Yucatan. To its credit, the relics found below the water's surface, provided much of what we know about Maya sacrifices.

All Maya ruins are compared to Chichen Itza, as for example was Mayapan. My personal recommendation is to spend time at as many of those other ruins on the Yucatan as possible. Chichen Itza with over two million visitors per year, is now the *Hard Rock Concert* of all Maya sites and a matter of taste.

GRUTA BALANKANCHE

Gruta Balankanche, one the largest of caves in the Yucatan, was hidden just off-road until 1959. Just 6 kilometres (3.7 miles) from Chichen Itza, it was related to *Maya Worship of the Underworld* and as a ceremonial site it represents one of the most important archaeological discoveries of recent times.

When these chambers were opened, ceremonial artifacts were revealed, found as they had been left hundreds of years ago. The advertised light and sound show in the present day consisted of bad acoustics and a lit pathway. However, when surrounded with an incredible number of ceramics laid there as offerings to *Maya Worship of the Underworld Gods*, the experience of viewing was positive.

Over two kilometres from the entrance to the underground is the *Balam Throne* with a stalagmite formation that resembled a large and sacred ceiba tree.

We were a group of four people, plus the required guide. As these were antique artifacts, he was as much a security guard as a guide. He spoke no English and the required decision for language was to do with the tape that would be played as we proceeded through. It was a wonderful experience with contemplation of Maya philosophy relating to the artifacts.

An area further on, deeper on circular steps - allowed us to view the offerings to the gods of the underworld from the Late Preclassic period of 300 BC, to the Early Classic period of 300 AD. Many of the objects are small duplicates of manos and metates (the implements used for grinding corn) as seen in the photo. In spite of the sacrifice on my part, my personal cut on the head, I highly recommend it - not forgetting to duck, but seeing this astounding Maya worship cave.

When we left a few hours later, the parking lot was still almost empty. There were two other cars along side of ours. It seems that caves may not be on the typical tour bus agenda - but it was an incredible adventure.

CENOTES

A cenote is a natural shaft that follows from the collapse of the ground into an underground river. They often provide the only source of fresh water and they became places of worship to gods of the Maya Underworld. There are 2400 studied and registered cenotes on the Yucatan peninsula. Access is usually aided by steps, often sculpted into the rock.

From visiting the cenotes of Dzibilchaltun (Xlacah), Yokdzonot and Ik Kil we understood how busy they could be. Other much advertised cenotes are: San Ignacio, Chelentun, Suytun, Chansinic'che, Bolonchoojol, Chihuan, X'Keken, Samula, Cenotillo, Dzul-ha, Dzitnup O Xkeken, Hubiku and more each year; all with large international crowds. In driving through the countryside after our Gruta Balankanche experience, we came upon a lesser advertised cenote. We had time for a swim.

As we compared the wonderful cave that we were swimming in - we concluded that they are not advertised in pecking order. It is easy to be swayed by the fact that cenotes as underground rivers are a fact of nature, forgetting that these are a part of the tourist industry. It does seem that everyone that has swum in a cenote will justify their choice as being *the very best.* Perhaps swimming in any of them is a wonderful experience with no exceptions.

Palomitas Cenote was far superior in beauty to Yokdzonot and others found in local magazines. Change rooms, lockers and towel rentals were available. We chose one of three stairways, each with their own ledge and stairway to the water. Only one other party was in the fairly large cave with us and they were using a different stairway access with its own ledge. Many cenotes are open to the sky, but this one only had one small hole, much like a skylight to the sun. As our eyes adjusted to the dimly lighted natural auditorium, we could see the incredible blues of the clean, clear water, at a depth of 150 feet.

Many contrasts of exotic hues can be found in these caves. *Palomitas Cenote* will always be remembered. It is a part of *Cenotes Aqua Dulce Aventuras* and is advertised by a couple of road signs as such. They are expanding their enterprise with a new restaurant, other caverns and a subdivision with building lots now for sale. It will not be off the beaten path for long, but we also concluded that as we had taken a short-cut side road, we would probably never be able to find it again.

Rio Lagartos

We drove back to our beach house by way of two interesting towns. Rio Lagartos is one of the most northern on the Yucatan Strait. It is a tourist town *want-to-be*. It looked like a beach party town, it was ready for the *flip-flop crowd*, but no tourists were there. The would-be guides were attempting to get our attention as we drove around, but most of the small businesses were vacant or not open. They mostly shouted that they wanted to show us the flamingoes.

A large biosphere reserve with 395 different bird species is near Rio Lagartos - with formations called *rias* (waterways from the ocean through mangroves). The largest group of flamingoes on the Yucatan is also just east of the town. The beach was a unique shade of red, but we had seen other red coloured lagoons, due to a high concentration of salt, near our beach home.

***

San Felipe

The second town nearby was San Felipe, a beautiful town. It was one of the few beach towns with houses built of wood, primarily with 2" X 12" boards. These *beach shacks* had a wonderful look. They had been recently painted. No garbage on the streets indicated that there were no issues with poverty, that is, none outwardly shown.
Unfortunately their malacon sported only two restaurants and one small hotel. There were no alternatives to the small sheds as housing, but it would be a very nice setting if something is ever built. I had seen these exact styles before in the fishing tackle huts of what is now the Malecon of Puerto Vallarta in the 1970's. They are also prevalent on the coast in Costa Rica as housing.

Probably due to the flatness of the roads, the three wheeled bikes, shown in the photo, are very common in all of the small towns of the Yucatan. They facilitate carrying entire families, are used as taxis and seemed to work well for hauling fairly large loads.

We dined at the only open restaurant near the beach, the few people we met were very cordial to us - and the town of San Felipe will be remembered as having its own picturesque character. It will be interesting to see if it also evolves into a Puerto Vallarta due to similarities.

* * *

TENTH WEEK:

Negative for Mexico, but positive for our us, was the fact that the Mexican peso had been devalued by sixteen percent as compared to the Canadian dollar since our arrival. We felt sad about it, but as a semi-retired couple we were much more comfortable with the cost of many services. Local vendors do not immediately adjust prices in comparison to international currency and as always in Mexico, we only used pesos.

In buying tickets to view a couple of cenotes, it seemed hilarious that Canadian Dollars were on the price list. Over the years I have often seen American Dollars listed, but I really did not think that Canadians wanted to pay say fifteen percent more in order to use *dollars from home*. I have laughed at individuals, who would declare from their travels that, "They really liked American Dollars there". I knew the added cost.

Canadians are now traveling here from the cruise ships for the day. Apparently this is not enough time to understand the exchange rate. One cafeteria did quite well as I watched them charge $15.00 CAD (conveniently a five and a ten dollar bill) for everything. The prices should have varied and the cost should have worked out to be one-half of that in pesos. I smiled when I actually heard one tourist sitting down and declaring, *"They sure like Canadian Dollars here."*

With plans to drive to the Caribbean and various points on the Riviera Maya, we relaxed for a week at our beach home. We would then stay for a few days at Playa del Carmen. To date none of the wonderful towns of the Yucatan Peninsula would satisfy our personal list of needs for a retirement home, something we considered possible. As much as we enjoyed our beach living in Uaymitun, the winds often came up in the afternoon and reminded us of our vulnerability to nature.

Our lifestyle was found to be a bit ridiculous here though, as we opened our fridge freezer this week to observe crab legs, three types of fresh fish fillets, bags of large prawns, and two lobsters. Purchased from our local fish vendor, the costs were less than one-third compared to Canada.

We enjoyed a *Carmenere* (red) wine by Zalacain from Chile that was seven years old, found at 99 pesos in *Ake Mercado*. As I had returned to buy the last (2010) four bottles in stock, we will have to now default to a four year old wine by the same vintner. We hope it is as perfect as the seven year old wine. In actual fact, I may have never purchased a good seven year old wine in my life before.

We had a visitor last night, the third of his family to visit. He had bright orange blotches on his mangy fur and I'm just presuming that the decorative style in the tropics has to do with being the male gender. It was a very ugly wild pig, also called a bush pig. Probably a juvenile he had wandered into our oceanfront patio. With each visit we had looked up from reading or watching television to see one snorting about in search of food. The lights have always been on and the timing is the same at about 9:00 pm. They are quite brazen as they have come right up to our glass sliding doors and are not deterred by the lights. I concluded in jest, that they were there to confirm that we really were in a rural setting. They had nothing to do with the fine wine.

The bush pigs are so distastefully ugly, I thought that I would insert an iguana posing instead.

This iguana lives with us and its mate, in our storage area - we like him because he eats insects.

We think that the wild pig might eat - us.

***

ELEVENTH WEEK:

The drive to **Playa del Carmen** was without incident, even as we were driving from one ocean to another (*gulf to sea*). Visiting the large city of Cancun was out, as cities were not logically on our itinerary on a trip like this. We were now used to the streets and avenues both being called *calle* with either odd or even numbers, so we could make sense of our city maps. That having been said, we *cheated* and used Google Maps for directions to our hotel for our arrival.

In Playa del Carmen our hotel was just off 5th Avenue, which was the main tourist service street for not just this city, but the surrounding areas. We dined, shopped, drank and danced until late. It was all possible with security and many street lights. This is probably the most international of cities in Mexico. Most European languages may be heard within a city block's walk. French seemed dominant with German being second. We were there five days and we enjoyed it immensely.

* * *

The Island of Cozumel could be viewed from the rooftop swimming pool at our hotel. I had stayed on the island for one week (also in 1974) and had then enjoyed the look of the rural plantations, the deserted beaches and the fact that at that time no cars were allowed on the island except taxis. The largest building in the small town of San Miguel was two stories high. We had rented a moped for the week and had circled the quiet island a few times.

From our rooftop meridor, we now looked out to view the new skyline of Cozumel. It was like any big city in the world at night. Highrises and their lights dominated the entire panorama of the island.

This is a quote from one of my other eBooks, *One Hundred Travel Moments (in 42 Countries)*.

"On the island of Cozumel, in Mexico in the early seventies, while staying for Christmas at what was then a small fishing village, on an island of seven kilometres by eleven kilometres - just before the explosion of luxury hotels in the area - *I ate the last giant turtle in Mexico.*

Well, perhaps that is a rumor I started among my Mexican friends. We enjoy the humor of it. At the time, as tourists are prone to do, we miscalculated the opening hours of the restaurants and the one small grocery store on Christmas day. By two o'clock in the afternoon I thought I was going to starve. Fortunately at about three o'clock a small beachside restaurant opened. They had a limited menu, but assured me that I would like turtle steak - especially for my Christmas dinner.

I had tasted turtle soup in France. The amount of actual turtle meat in it was minimal. It was not even a spoonful of meat. These local islanders were suggesting a serving of actual steak from a turtle apparently just caught that morning.

I went for it. Not only was this a large portion of steak covering the entire plate, but it was absolutely tasty. With a consistency a bit like pork when it is roasted perfectly, with a subtlety of wild seafood and a delicacy of spices that enhanced and still allowed the taste of turtle to shine through, I remember it being exotic in every bite.

As time went by and killing giant turtles became illegal, and more importantly conversations were about the rarity of large turtles, I would smile with guilt as I would reflect on the simple fact that I may have eaten the last giant turtle in Mexico. Exaggeration can be fun with travel stories."

I now chose not to visit Cozumel a second time as the expression that *you can't go back* would obviously be true. It would have been easy to visit, as there is a fast ferry consistently leaving from Playa del Carmen, allowing a couple of thousand people per day to view the *tropical island paradise*.

* * *

Puerto Morelos was a must see for us. We wanted to see what had been represented as the perfect retirement community. The town square, the views of the Caribbean, the expat community, the weather and anything else that seemed idyllic for retirement could be added to a list - and it did exist just as statistics would verify.

It was stated in at least two memoirs of expats living there, that the *Mexicans lived on the other side of the highway*. The shock was that the standard of living on the other side was by my estimation, the poorest in all of Mexico. In contrast, the standard of living and quality of construction, on the Caribbean side, was luxury.

Highway #302 cutting through the two, created the chaotic atmosphere of big city driving on both sides. In that Puerto Morelos is now sandwiched between Cancun and Playa del Carmen - it is just a matter of time until it becomes a part of one of the two cities. Idyllic it is no longer, however we returned a second day and *hung-out*, just to be sure about our negative assessment.

We hired a small boat and the pilot showed us the coastline of Puerto Morelos and more importantly the coral reef. Called the *Great Mesoamerican Reef* and running south as far as Belize, it is second in size only to the *Great Barrier Reef* of Australia.

It was a day without wind and therefore we could view the coral as if we were snorkeling. I recommend snorkeling, but we had driven around and now our daylight was limited. The coral was often one foot or so from ocean level and as the water was perfectly clear, we could enjoy the experience of seeing this massive reef just below us. A glass bottom boat wasn't a requirement with this perfect view. This couple of hours was well worth the few pesos.

***

9 TULUM, Quintana Roo

The management of Tulum accomplished what the Chichen Itza INAH had not. The same massive crowds existed, but inside the old walls of this city there were no sales people crying out for customers. The walk from the parking lot to the ruins may be about one kilometre or half a mile and there are many kiosks of Mexican souvenirs within that section. But within the old walls of the site, the crowds were orderly and each person seemed to politely respect the ambiance of the occasion. The row of people was enormous, moving along almost single file. It was at a slow pace so everyone would not miss anything that this once Maya port town offered.

Small coastal centres like Tulum controlled the sea routes that united the Yucatan with the Gulf of Mexico and the ports in Honduras and Nicaragua. It was compared to the city of Seville, Spain in size, upon the first viewing by the Spanish in 1518. An open flame at the top of the Castle, one of the main structures and the highest, was then visible as a navigational aid.

The Maya buildings, foundations and worship shrines were visually superseded by the landscape and the incredible Caribbean blues and turquoises. One of the most photographed sites, it did not let us down with its natural beauty. If the perfection of the day visiting manicured green terrain and appreciating the perfectly blue sky were not enough, we were able to go for a quick dip in the Caribbean. The beach area, also within the site, was not large, but the massive crowd seemed to fit themselves into the beach area as if planned.

The main structures on this site are:
- The Castle,
- The Temple of the Wind,
- The Temple of the Paintings,
- The Temple of the Descending God,`
- The surrounding Walls are a formative structure.

* * *

It seemed logical to explore the town of Tulum as this was a part of the *Maya Riviera* that we had heard about for years, both for retirement and for all-inclusive vacations. After driving about the town of Tulum (*Tulum Pueblo*) now renamed *Central Tulum*, we toured the middle area now called *Aldea Zama*, now advertised as the *Heart of Tulum*. The ruins were formerly know by the name of Zama, meaning *city of dawn* due to its sunrises. The land developers here have replicated the name.

The new naming of areas did not make sense to us until we drove to the beach of Tulum. On the Caribbean side of town this new middle area, mostly under construction, is between the beach and *Central Tulum*. The town of Tulum is about to be massive. The number of apartments under construction is enormous, with roads in, presales existing and bike paths to the beach ready-to-go.

We happened to see a real estate zoning map. The beach area is now designated *Hotel Zone* (if translated to English). Presently the rambling and crude shelters that have often been described as *Hippy Heaven* are made up of small buildings with no running water and no sewer system. But Tulum's stretch of low population beach is about to be another issue of the past.

Thus we were able to reach a conclusion. We had arrived in Playa del Carmen not knowing what to expect. We now could see that from Cancun in the north to Tulum in the south, the entire area of the *Riviera Maya* replicated the centre of the state of Florida, USA (as I searched for examples). It was now entirely big city living or about to be. On the positive that includes the best types of restaurants, sophisticated beach clubs and wonderful but expensive views. On the negative, we were in the wrong age group for the big city and had left city life purposely. In leaving, we felt we were going to our beach home on the Yucatan as something much more palatable.

* * *

Coba was only 50 kilometres (31 miles) from Tulum and it was an easy stop, facilitating a one day drive back to our beach home. I could relax and drive on paved country roads again.

10 COBA, Quintana Roo

Coba is in a wooded forest and the massive site is spread out with walking and bicycle paths through the shade of its trees. We chose to walk, not just enjoying the site, but giving us a chance to appreciate the terrain, the woods and anything else we might be surprised at. Rented bikes were popular, as bicycle speed on the level road system was probably more logical than walking.

Once home to 50,00 people, Coba did not decline until the 14th century, at which time a massive revolt destroyed much of it. *Nohoch Mul*, Yucatan's highest pyramid is here at a height of 42 metres (138 feet). The pyramid is popular as it is one of the few where climbing it is still allowed. Hundreds, if not thousands of tourists each day, stand on its stairs with arms outstretched, waiting for a photo, as if the only person to have posed in that manner.

The stelae seen here establishes its founding in 600 AD, but because of the earlier era of construction, it has no developed styles. It is the height of the pyramid that allows its rivalry with other major sites where much more artistic merit exists. In fact it might seem as a great mound of rock rubble in comparison.

Glyphs may be seen under protected roofing throughout the site, but they are not as identifiable or clear as at other ruins.

Xaibe Palace seems to be unique in that its corners are rounded so much that it seems circular. Coba is also known for its massive sakbe'oob (road) system, actually totalling forty, and this structure is in the converging centre of four. Less than 15 metres (50 feet) high, its circular shape seems so unique making the trip necessary, when doing the rounds of Maya ruins. It is the round structure that I will remember best from Coba.

The main structures on this site are:
- Xaibe Palace,
- The (small) Ball Court,
- Nochoch Mul,
- The Church,
- The Paintings Group, and
- The many free standing stelae.

*　*　*

TWELFTH WEEK:

It's amazing that a house can become a home so easily. It may have been that I was happy to get out of the road traffic of the Caribbean Coast. We did what people around the world usually do. We shopped for groceries. It is interesting that as a Canadian we have found it very natural to shop for food in Mexico. Perhaps this is because a standard of good quality food exists around the world.

Third world countries are different, but Mexico is not a third world country any longer. We had driven through too many small towns on the Yucatan, and viewed the young people with their school uniforms, busily hurrying to and from various lessons, to think otherwise. The education process was also destroying the terrible class system that existed in full force until only a few years ago. It is easy to believe in Mexico and the future of Mexico. It is easy to feel saddened by *American racism* as it surfaces in the political news.

Life on the beach means that the issue of sand fleas is prevalent. I googled it. They are of two types, crustacea (not an insect) and arthropod (an insect). Enough information - their bites are uncomfortable. After a few weeks, I concluded that the trick is to walk below the high tide line - where they can't reside. That idea alone allowed us to walk on this wonderful beach of the Gulf of Mexico - unbitten - for awhile.

It was a lousy theory. Sorry about the bad advice. I still get bitten and I finally gave in to using more spray.

***

The Regional Museum of Anthropology in Merida visit was an easy find as it's on Paseo de Montejo, the main street entering the city from our area on the north.

The museum was built in 1909 and is filled with ceramics providing an overview of the Maya World of the Yucatan. As a museum of anthropology it's in a perfect setting within the elaborate splendor of a former mansion.
This museum of anthropology is not toured by a definable ratio of tourists as compared to the ruins. We shared our experiences here with less than twenty others, which is too bad, as many of the better kept artifacts of many types are displayed in this museum. They were taken away from the ruins for safety and preservation.

The first museum that we visited, a couple of months prior, was enjoyed by more tourists, that being the contemporary *El Gran Museo del Mundo Mayo*, coincidentally just down the same street.

***

THIRTEENTH WEEK:

We now simply enjoyed a second or third visit to the ruins close by, along with our ongoing life on the beach.

Overhead we are often treated to the effortless soaring of *Great Frigatebirds*. With up to an eight foot wingspan and very little movement they gracefully seem to stay stationary and then change altitude as if to show their skill against our harsh afternoon winds - flying over two thousand metres high. We have seen them fly near the water and scoop up airborne flying fish, as if being served by a large spoon on a plate. Being black and silent they have often been called *Pirate Birds*.

Other much smaller birds have fluttered within our yard. A tiny Sheartail likes to land on the bougainvillea just outside our kitchen window. Bright Orange Orioles, vivid blue Indigo Bunting Birds, Scarlet Tanagers, a sweet sounding striped grey and white bird called a Brown-breasted Flycatcher, are all a part of our life. It seems that nature is good to the people of the Yucatan Peninsula.

***

FOURTEENTH WEEK:

The Gulf of Mexico often treated us to a show of various hues of green and blue. In the morning, as we sipped our second coffee on the patio, an emerald tint with beige from the sand was often dominant near the shore. A royal blue formed the outline on the horizon.

The show began with the wind becoming a bit harsher. The blue of the horizon would slowly progress towards us. We could watch the progression until finally the entire gulf was a vivid blue. The emerald and beige would dissipate.

A lighter shade of emerald green would then begin as streaks towards the horizon. It would recede towards us until the entire gulf was emerald, with no blues in sight. The cycle would continue with a presentation of navy blue in a straight horizontal line, coming towards us.

Other days began with a glass mirror sea that was a vivid blue. Looking through the palm trees, it was like a photo card or a travel brochure. The Gulf of Mexico water is not as clear nor is it as pretty as the turquoise of the Caribbean, but it has its moments.

* * *

FIFTEENTH WEEK:

Planning a trip to the *Puuc Route,* the area of Uxmal, Labna, Kabah, Sayil and Xlapak was exciting, as life on the beach was becoming *overly normal*.

We had already visited Edzna, often included in the Puuc Route, and realized that these sites were each unusual. Archaeological writings had clearly stated that these last few Puuc sites in our plan are even more perfect as architecture. As usual we booked our hotel online and due to what seemed to be a fraction of hotel costs in Canada, we decided to stay six days.

I had now learned about the cycle of nature that palm trees easily teach. The lower branches die, one by one, coinciding with a new branch sprouting from the tree centre at its top. I had never witnessed this process, as I had only visited locations with tropical palms for short periods. Resorts, for example, consistently trim their trees, probably before the morning begins for most visitors. Here, it seemed to be my duty to cut off the large dead branches, even as a tenant. I learned that tending to a tropical garden can be quite satisfying and fun.

However, after four months, I learned that this was ongoing. One had to cut off the dead branches *forever*. The novelty wore off and I concluded that maybe condos with a maintenance man were not such a bad idea.

There seemed to be a bit of irony in that the owner visited us only one time. He thought that he should come and cut and take away the dead palm branches. He was nice enough to phone ahead, assuring me that he didn't have to enter our rented home. *He was just going to clean up the landscape with a small crew.* Later under the palms, when I enquired about his occupation, he stated that he was a *professional landscaper*. I'm glad he had liked my work, at least seemed to.

* * *

SIXTEENTH WEEK:

Swimming in the local cenotes was a pleasure and a part of nature. We had no shortage of access to that entertainment, although nature could be creative in its provisions. With an appreciation of nature, Martha had returned quickly from the storage area patio with an unusual proclamation. "There's a scorpion in the patio. He's huge."

"I'll put my sandals on," as if I knew what to do next.

The scorpion left the inside patio area and proceeded across the area of cobblestones in the outside yard.

"I guess I should kill him." I was searching for some kind of logic. "I'll use my shovel." I went to the storage and got out my armament.

Whack! "I missed, he's still walking."

I calculated the roundness of the shovel. Whack!

"Good, he's two dimensional." I scraped him to the side towards the fence.

"He was like a small animal. Huge for an insect, but very beautiful. It was the way he walked - so elegantly with that large tail swaying in the air. Beautiful!" Martha was very positive about the entire experience.

"I like him two dimensional," I asserted.

* * *

SEVENTEENTH WEEK:

Finally we are on the *Puuc Route* in the area often referred to as the Puuc hills. We drove past our hotel early and purposely arrived at the most advertised of chocolate museums, across from the gates of the archaeological centre of Uxmal. We had not visited the numerous chocolate museums scattered along our route, as we presumed that none were necessarily authentic. They were mostly designed to sell chocolate. It seemed necessary to make an exception of this largest one. We were correct in our assumption and we spent an enjoyable two and one-half hours on the museum grounds. As unusual as it may seem to explore the history of something like cocoa, it was simply fun. The total name is *Eco Park Chocolate Museum, Uxmal*.

***

The Grutas de Loltun was not far from the Puuc cities, and less than one hour from our hotel. Very few travelers were on the road, and we toured the cave with one other couple and a mandatory tour guide - as a great asset.

The Grutas Loltun is one of the largest caves on the Peninsula. The 2 kilometre (1.5 mile) cave complex that we toured, has the longest history of human habitation in the Yucatan. It was confirmed as having a beginning in 9000 BC. Ceramics were found from as early as 3000 BC. As the Maya began to build houses in about 300 AD, the cave was no longer used to provide shelter.

As a natural phenomenon of massive *rooms*, it was easy walking. It has exposed, bizarre rock formations, and a couple of ancient relics with fresco paintings along the walls. The bones of horses, camels, deer and other mammals that have been extinct for over fourteen thousand years - have have been found in this cave. The wonderful art work is from an earlier period dating between 1200 BC and 400 BC. Of the *Olmec* culture, which preceded Mayan civilization, It is now displayed a few metres from where it was found in the Grutas Loltun.

11 LABNA, Yucatan

On the return trip from the Grutas Loltun, at Labna, a very compact site, we stopped, entered and immediately viewed the Palace on the left of the entry. It was impressive and was obvious as a *Puuc* design with geometric symbols and shapes. Here was architecture at its finest, some from 300 AD, most from 700 AD. We paused and enjoyed the inspiring visual moments.

Proceeding to the pyramid known as El Mirador (the lookout, or Watchtower), then to the Great Palace, we now knew that this was not a minor ruin. A smaller settlement, between 750 and 1000 people, the population was never over 2500. Puuc architecture had won us over. What we will not forget is the large arch known as the *Labna Arch.* It seemed like the most perfect Arch of the Maya World.

Showing the need to make constant references to the numerous influences within ruined cities, this arch is no exception. From the front, the upper area is made up of *Chaac Masks* arranged near the corners. These appear above a frieze of stylized serpent carvings. The painted remains of tufts of quetzal feathers may be seen in green and blue. From the rear, the facade is decorated only with frets, and a series of *Puuc* columns and small squares, which form stylized masks.

Like many buildings of the Maya World, there are a least two theories of its existence. The arch may have been the main entrance to the *sache*, the highway to Uxmal, or it may have been a division between the two quadrangles of structures in this great example of urban planning.

We viewed it from every direction possible, photographed it, walked around it - and simply hated to leave. No structure, along with many detailed embellishments, built or designed within the last fourteen hundred years, could be more emotionally inspiring.

12 XLAPAC, Yucatan

This site of fourteen unrestored mounds and three partially restored pyramids allowed us to view the condition of the sites when they were discovered by Europeans. All that is needed is an *Indiana Jones Hat* and good walking shoes. The style of hat is optional.

Viewing partially restored sites with this type of jungle foliage allows the feeling of exploration, and it is easy to forget that many visitors have come before us. We, at least, are discovering it, for the very first time.

There are a total of three groups of structures and much left unknown - built between 750 and 1000 AD. The Palace is the most restored structure with a complete front facade.

***

13 SAYIL, Yucatan

The two main structures in Sayil, built from 750 AD, are:
- The Great Palace, where a sache starts directly from the square below; and
- A small square temple, the El Mirador (or the Lookout).

Sayil exhibits open spaces and clean architectural lines of the Puuc style.

Three stories high, with a large number of bas-reliefs, the palace included ninety bedrooms for approximately three-hundred and fifty people. The columns were noticeably different. With two columns in each doorway, these were like Mediterranean architecture, in that they had *Doric* square capitals. The capitals facilitated a header above the door, but to me they seemed out of place in the Mexico of the Maya. I needed to remember that diversity and creativity in design are important elements of architecture.

Sayil features a very small outdoor museum protected by a thatched roof near the entrance to the site. There seemed to be a system related to the price of admission.

As a guess, the price was in ratio to popularity. Sayil was one of the few at zero admission. Due to the magnificent views of structures, the size of these massive ruins and the maintenance required - we found all of the tickets to every site to be a bargain.

***

14 KABAH, Yucatan

The main structures from 700 AD on this site are
- The Kodz Poop (or Temple of the Masks),
- The Great Palace,
- The Great Temple (an oval pyramid called Teocalli),
- The large Arch

The large Arch connects a sacbe or causeway to the corresponding arch at Uxmal.

The facade of the *Kodz Poop* building is made up of more than 250 representations of Chaac, the Maya Rain God. In an attempt to emphasize the ornate of this building, writers have often used the word *baroque*. It is difficult to make a statement about the elaborate design and detail of Kodz Poop. Nowhere in the world is there a facade more embellished.

The structure may be everyone's favourite architecturally integrated design. The spelling varies as it is often *Codz Poop*.

None of the sites on the *Puuc Route* were viewed with more than five other visitors at a time. For some reason there were no large tour buses in contrast to the more northern Maya Ruins. We braced ourselves for a much different experience in Uxmal - like the circus of Chichen Itza.

***

15 UXMAL, Yucatan

There is something significant about experiencing a ruined city at the start of one's adult life - and again after retirement. It has to do with the eternal aspect of the ruins themselves. Our adult lives are but a flash in comparison, however, our *adult one-half century* actually has a moment of relevance when held up to the one-thousand years. For this I felt a kinship with Uxmal.

This incredible ruined city has been ingrained within my inner-conscious for most of my life. I had climbed the *Pyramid of the Magician* in my youth and had enjoyed its quiet ambiance of history. But it was the architecture that was an inspiration lasting a lifetime. In the seventies the art of Uxmal had changed me. I have related to the arts differently for the period, perhaps knowing that over sixteen hundred years ago *art in architecture* mattered.

This trip, we had saved Uxmal for one full day of *hanging out* - just being there and viewing.

The main structures built from 500 AD, are:
- The Nun's Quadrangle, which has North, East, West and South Buildings,
- The smaller Birds Quadrangle,
- The large Pyramid (or Temple) of the Magician,
- The Cemetery Group,
- An unrestored Ball Court,
- A freestanding House of the Turtles,

- The Palace of the Governor,
- The facade of the House of the Pigeons, (a former Quadrangle, or the Dovecote),
- The Great Pyramid,
- The unrestored Old Woman's House.

A mix of architectural types is exemplified on the site, with the Pyramid of the Magician being considered *Chenes* in style - the other structures being *Puuc*. Otherwise it followed the pattern of Classic Maya pyramids, which were constructed on a series of narrowing, tapered platforms with a temple on top. The pyramid here again, was an artistic device, designed to make the Temple, on top, appear much like a cave.

Like many visitors, we prefered the visual feast of the *Palace of the Governor.* However Uxmal in general is a most wonderful visual experience of departed greatness. Hundreds of years have passed since its conception, but by the standards of any era, antique and modern, Uxmal is incredible in its town planning, design emphasis and homage to the people that lived there.

One of the reasons to compare the sites is that their roles as political and religious centres changed through history. In general the role of Uxmal, from the 7th to the 9th centuries was comparable to that of Chichen Itza between the 9th and 11th. Mayapan dominated during the 12th and 13th centuries. Yet even having been built before these other two centres, Uxmal with the Puuc elements of design seems more modern.

Rather than duplicating the many detailed descriptions of all of these structures all well presented elsewhere, I will state that emotionally the entire Uxmal ruin provides food for thought as a learning experience. This has to do with the proof of the tangibility of time.

The tourist retail centre includes restaurants and shops. It is adjacent, but outside of the gate to the ruins, and is not in any way like that of Chichen Itza. We enjoyed browsing, buying a few quality books, and relaxing with some of the local input into archeology. A photo presentation centre of the reconstruction process and hard labour in the sun, is displayed in the best of taste. It confirmed that it was okay for me to believe that if only one Maya ruin was to be experienced, it should be Uxmal.

Our hotel overlooked the ruins of Uxmal offering quite a panorama. But the fact of being close offered us a night light show provided by nature. In the Yucatan, dark clouds float in the foreground of the evening sky, with sun-lit clouds providing the background. For that reason, the shadows in the sky were unreal to us. However the mystery of the ancient Maya World seemed more enhanced by both sheet-lightning and scattered lightning bolts - all directly above the ruins of Uxmal. The rain held off and lightning prevailed. We sat relaxing on our hotel balcony and visually went back in time to the magic of one thousand years before.

Uxmal had provided us with a visual feast of architectural splendor during the day. Now at dusk, with sun rays and lightning bolts, it was providing an exotic farewell message. Perhaps that meant the we had to return some day. Perhaps, the Maya Gods were speaking.

* * *

EIGHTEENTH WEEK:

A black chicken from next door is still visiting us every day. She strolls into our yard, as chickens do, inspects our car, which seems strange, and finally pecks away at the clumps of grass growing in the sand. Both our front and backyard are sand.

Everywhere that I've stayed in Mexico has the sound of a rooster crowing. The only exceptions have been in the cities. Unfortunately, here the rooster is next door and he never stops crowing. Usually the wind muffles his irritating sound and we have gotten used to both the wind and the crowing.

A great writer wrote that, "Men go to war because the women are watching." To my amazement the rooster is quiet when the black chicken visits. I wonder if there is a tie-in. No chicken to show off to, and no crowing. I must be getting bored.

Writing is an ideal avocation in semi-retirement. I enjoy it. Relaxing is not a bad thing: *Life is a Beach*.

* * *

NINETEENTH WEEK:

Our last and most adventure-some road trip took us to Chicanna Ecovillage Resort in the small town of Xpujil. We stayed for six days here, near the *Biosphere of Calakmul*, bordering on Guatemala. We planned to drive to Chetumal on the border of Belize.

We drove by Campeche using the toll road of the past misadventure. There were no incidences here, and if there were, I had promised myself that I would not *ask for change*.

***

The ruins now visited were primarily the *Rio Bec* architectural style of the Late Classic period of 600 AD to 900 AD. It is the most unusual of Maya architectural styles. The sixty sites in the region are characterized by towers creating a strong emphasis on verticality.

In many cases, the steps on these towers are mostly ornamental and are too small to be used, or are adorned by huge masks.

The entrances were most often designed to represent the open jaws of the Earth Monster.

* * *

16 BALAMKU, Campeche

The city of Balamku was inhabited from 600 BC to 1000 AC, Not a lot of research or writing has been done on this site as the books that I found, on standard book shelves, at museums or tourist outlets, did not mention it. Balamku (also spelled Balam-ku) should not be confused with Balam Kuk in Chiapas.

As I finally gazed in wonderment at the beauty of this jungle ruin, I wondered again if most tourist guide books were plagiarism. If one book missed a site like this, did many others later leave it out, due to sheer copying? I can only presume so.

We had made good time in the trip to the most southern portion of the Yucatan Peninsula and could project our arrival at our hotel to be before dark. This allowed our first day in the area to be finished off with what we presumed must be both a small site and a non eventful viewing. It was only three kilometres (two miles) off the highway.

At Balamku and in viewing the Temple of the Friezes, we saw a most dynamic stucco frieze. Sheltered from the elements permanently it was a perfect reminder to why we had ventured to this area in the first place.

Representing the Earth Monster and the Maya Underworld, it was a view truly unique in Maya design. The painted areas of the friese are exquisitely preserved. Besides illustrating the opposite and complementary aspects of the Underworld, the friese compares dynastic and solar cycles. The king rises from the earth monster's paw, just as the Sun emerges from the Earth's mouth. The king's death is then shown as a sunset, as he falls into the monster's mouth.

An amphibian also rises from the Earth Monster's cleft and from its mouth the king emerges. The large masks and jaguars express the wealth of the earth and the amphibian assures transition between these two worlds. The frieze indicates the nature and the function of the building where it belongs - the upper level corresponds to the earth's surface and the substructure is the Underworld.

Entering through one of the doors you are penetrating the Underworld.

***

17 CALAKMUL, Campeche

Exploring this ruin in the jungle, about fifteen kilometres from the border of Guatemala, we felt the exhilaration of pure adventure. One of the largest Maya cities of the Late Preclassic and Classic periods, Calakmul covers 70 square kilometers (27 square miles). It is located in the Calakmul Biosphere Reserve and is famous for having more than 100 engraved stelae showing richly dressed figures. We found them there, scattered over the entire site. The jungle has encroached, with trees even entwining and circling the stelae. This was a reality of Maya *ruin hopping* that we thought we might achieve and that we thought we could only hope for.

Calakmul was the traditional rival of Tikal in Guatemala and her allies and was also known for many military clashes against Palenque. As can be imagined, it is an enormous city where archaeologist are currently unearthing extraordinary remains.

The northern limits of the lowlands of the Maya were marked by the area of influence of this metropolis of Calakmul, now in the south of the state of Campeche. A development of the individual style of architecture here, due to the remote and early origin, may be found at Calakmul.

To get there is an adventure. We saw no tour buses and only a few cars were to be seen once having arrived. Over sixty kilometres (37 miles) of paved road, almost in a straight line, took almost two hours to navigate. That's because of the pot holes. Some are of the size that would welcome a front tire, taking it down to a depth restrained only by the car's frame. It seemed that any speed might wreak a front end completely. My driving was never in a *straight line*.

The necessity for a slower speed was offset by occasional views of wildlife. We saw more small animals and birds on this day, than through the entire five months on the Northern Yucatan. We were in the *Calakmul Biosphere Reserve* and it proved its worth in viewing.

Even in later exiting the site on foot, we walked within a cloud of butterflies, as if to accentuate that fact. The spider monkey was an occasional visitor, at home in the ruined city.

There were also many wild turkeys sometimes called *Hacienda Chickens*, along the route. It seems that the tropics have been good to these birds, with not a grey feather in sight. We were content not to see the jaguars that still inhabit this area. This plump wild turkey probably was also. He posed for me at the side of the road, then attempted to attack the car, gave up and fled.

There were no maps available at the entrance. We wanted to make sure that we saw the largest of the most elaborate structures. What we did not know was that here it was simply named *Building II*. We followed the signs to the *Grand Acropolis*, and like many visitors, almost missed the most impressive of the pyramids in Calakmul.

The onsite maps showed all of the structures, but what they did not describe was that *Building II* was the *grand-daddy* of the them all. After more than two and one-half hours on the site and having viewed the *Grand Acropolis,* we had missed one single path.

Frustrated by knowing that we had not viewed the impressive pyramid shown in the bill-board advertising, we took another path, kept walking, persevered, rounded a corner and found it. Enormous, breathtaking and as we hoped, the steps were adorned on each side by huge masks - *Rio Bec* style.

We climbed to the top of Building II, the second highest structure in the ruined city, and in doing so, we gazed at Guatemala less than thirty kilometres (twenty miles) away. We all have reasons for being on a site, or at any tourist destination. To us it said we were at a specific place on a map. It was well worth the horrendous drive.

At the top, Martha, an avid climber, made the observation: "It is the first time in all of my travels that I have climbed to the top of a structure and for three-hundred and sixty degrees, can not see any modern civilization."

That was true, usually there's a cell tower, a road, or a building within the horizon. Here there was literally only jungle and ruins for the entire scope of visibility. That was the power of the Maya ruin of Calakmul to us on that particular day.

What I will refer to as a *condo development* was wonderful to climb about and explore. It was within the residential section of the ancient city and the layout struck my imagination. I want to believe that it was for a multi-generational family group, with the older folks having the permanent roofed rooms. The other roof tops were built of perishable material and did not last the one thousand years.

Back at our hotel, we spoke to a couple who had missed seeing *Building II*, had searched for a *Grand Acropolis* as the signs on the site had indicated. Like us they found that this was not the structure - and will forever wish they had persevered and found *Building II*. We chose to tell them that they really did *miss out*.

***

18 CHICANNA, Campeche

Built between 300 BC and 1150 AD in the period of Preclassical and Classical, the emphasis on this area was that it was an elitist residential suburb of Becan. The families living here were one step below royalty, one step above merchants. The city planners took advantage of the changes in elevations within their exceptional designs. The site was only discovered in 1966 and materials and artifacts from Guatemala and Honduras have recently been found.

The entrance carvings of the exquisite second structure had been rebuilt using the original material, however this is a time where we may wonder about the authenticity of refurbishing in the first place. The definitions of antique verses replicas usually are in ratio to the amount of new material. This is true of arms, swords, furniture and other antique items. A high ratio of new material renders them almost worthless in the retail marketplace. I don't know the answer to this ongoing definition within the Maya ruins, but it is a quandary.

But the large carved mask of Itzamna, the Earth Monster, was incredibly beautiful to view on both of these buildings.

* * *

19 XPUJIL, Campeche

Primarily built between 600 AD and 950 AD, Xpujil is sometimes referred to as Xpuil or Xpuhil, The locals refer to it as Xpujil. It is the location of the famous Building Number 1, a structure with three entrances and three towers. The unusual tower is at the centre, unusual because most *Rio Bec* Structures only have two roof combs. Each tower is 82 feet high and topped by an architectural crest in the form of a mask and open jaws, that surround a false entrance. The false stairways here are embellished with other large masks and are also a *Chenes* influenced style.

In the 1970's, Tatiana Proskouriakoff illustrated Structure I in perspective, showing that the three towers were not real temples, but solid masonry that appeared to have no functional use other than to break the rectangular contour of the total architectural image - a perfect *Rio Bec* example. We were fortunate to be able to climb, crawl through and touch the antique masonry. The false rooms and the stairways leading to nowhere in particular were real. The rendering is now in public domain, such that it is allowable as a reproduction.

* * *

20 BECAN, Campeche

The earliest archeological evidence here dates from 550 BC, when the *Olmec* culture was declining. Flourishing with both a large population and massive construction between 500 AD and 800 AD, Becan is a pure example of *Rio Bec* architecture. It was abandoned in 1200 AD.

The ruined city of Becan is unusual in that it has a trench or moat five metres deep, sixteen metres wide with a perimeter of two kilometres (1.5 miles approximately). The trench may be seen near the entrance. It encompasses twelve hectares, three of which may be visited. The platforms and foundations of the simpler homes of the ancient Maya are outside the visiting area of three hectares (2 square miles).

One of the largest Maya cities in the *Rio Bec* area, its two lateral towers and the two main plazas are the focal point of the structures.

* * *

21 DZIBANCHE. Quintana Roo

This large, though little known city was built from 200 AD onward. It was a ceremonial centre with plazas surrounded by pyramidal bases.

With a flaunting of open rooms, this pyramid showed with a flourish that no two Mayan cities were alike, they all had great personalities. The highest in Dzibanche, built from 600 AD, it has a temple with two magnificent galleries. The walls support a hollowed out trapezoidal cresting that holds three stuccoed masks. The temples pediments retain panels, four at the back and three on each side.

In the platform, which holds the temple, there are three vaulted chambers. One of the lower ones was found to contain the remains of the Lord of Dzibanche. The title is due to the importance of the funerary monument erected in his honor and to the richness of the offerings buried with him.

* * *

22 KINICHNA, Quintana Roo

I will personally remember Kinichna because of dehydration. I had never experienced it before. Upon occasion, I had felt a little dizzy while hiking. This was different. Possibly it built up over a three day period and was due a lack of adequate water intake each day.

In the morning it felt that I could not speak very well. By noon, I was completely tongue-tied. I quickly reviewed the possibilities by way of satellite on google. That was really breaking ranks with exploring *Maya Ruins technology*. When being unable to speak, I guess I have no pride. I read that the tongue swells up, hence the hampered speech. I began drinking water - a lot of water. It went away. As a matter of expression, *Trust me, drink a lot of water when exploring Maya Ruins*. I will from now on.

My only excuse is that I was thoroughly engrossed with enjoying the ruins.

We had observed many signs along the road to new ruins and Kinichna was a newly offered one. The ruin had been discovered long ago, however it is required that at least one staff member is available. *Ruin robbing* is to be a thing of the past as the National Institute of Anthropology (INAH - Mexico) provides the services of security. This was to be our example of a lesser ruin, in that not a lot was yet explored, or at least not uncovered.

The main pyramid was within view, with many unknown mounds of earth scattered around nearby, waiting to be explored. Only one side was exposed, the other three were dirt covered with overgrowth.

Many of the lesser ruins, marked only by arrows on the highway, are like this with only a part of one building exposed. As in all regions, there are many lesser known sites, also lesser known to us, the general public. These sites may have as few as one or two structures in various levels of erosion and decay. But unlike in the *Puuc* region, the ruins in the *Rio Bec* region retained their picturesque trees, even on the steps, and provided a feeling of *exploring the jungle.* The steps of Kinichna are a perfect example of work yet to be done.

***

My first realization of enjoying the presence of birds came about three years ago, in the jungles of Costa Rica. The birds that we enjoyed in the jungles of the Southern Yucatan Peninsula numbered over 846 species. It was quite an amazing sound at any given moment.

Our hotel, Chicanna Ecovillage, was able to boast 122 species of birds as full time residences within their grounds. They were all beautiful and unique.

***

We expected the ruggedness that usually exists in a border town and a sea port in Chetumal. What we saw, was one of the nicest ocean side cities anywhere. A park stretched along the city shore for the width of the city. Both sides of the street were bordered with beautiful buildings and public ocean side parks of both flora and fauna. Because of our expectations, and prejudiced thoughts - we were *in shock.* We had almost not bothered to drive into the city centre, but the beauty of the

Caribbean is here and it is a city to which you say that you have to return. It had a *wow factor* in looking out over the Caribbean Sea.

Traveling onward, we found that downtown Bacalar had a most beautiful lagoon. Seven different *Cenotes* surface within it. The lagoon behind our beach house could not be compared for tropical splendor. Ours was a standard blue. Here hundreds of tours per day in small boats were viewing its splendor. The vibrant blues and greens of the Caribbean coast thrived, framed by this incredible lagoon.

We observed that Bacalar was a town for youth by the number of fairly modern hostels advertised on the main street. Most of the tourists were twenty-something. I could understand why they were here with the beauty of the Caribbean.

* * *

After about a two hours drive back we viewed the *slash and burn system* of farming. The jungle is burnt, then after a couple of years of farming, the plot is left fallow to allow the regrowth of vegetation. It seems that without adequate equipment this is the only possible methodology. The system is aborted in most industrial or modern farming areas of Mexico.

There are three choices for returning from the area of Xpujil, we had chosen Highway 307, turning off to Miguel Hidalgo, then Highways 203 and 184 to Merida from Chetumal. In effect we were driving east to west at 45 degrees northward.

Along this route, we drove through some very rural *backwoods towns*, encountering two separate clusters of homes that should have belonged in the last century. The groups of houses represented unincorporated towns. Antiquated construction methods with vertical sticks, somewhat open to the air and using thatched roofs, were as we had seen on some of the museum grounds. Built of stick walls not necessarily straight, windows were not always necessary as the air blew nicely through. This type of thatched roofed, stick home, cannot be seen elsewhere on the Peninsula.

I make no judgement with this observation as my maternal grandparents lived on a homestead in a log cabin (I lived with them for three years). However leaving home to a residential school is probably necessary here, as I noticed that the one room school was small, and probably only went up to grade eight. I am aware of the younger generation's struggles in overcoming their parent's anti-establishment feelings, as they attempt to reinvent their lives. The youth here now have cell phones with internet and due to that influence they will (without a doubt) make an attempt to prosper.

Anti-establishmentism is difficult to explain unless we have experienced it. I will directly quote from John Lloyd Stephens in his 1843 writing, *Incidents of Travel in Yucatan*, still valid today.

"At the time of our visit, owing to the long continuance of rains, they furnished a sufficient supply for domestic use, but the people were not able to keep horses or cows, or cattle of any kind, the only animals they had being hogs.

In the dry season this source of supply failed them, the holes in the rocks were dry. They were obliged to send to a well, being half a mile under ground, and so steep that it was reached only by descending nine different staircases.

It seemed strange that any community should be willing to live where this article of primary necessity (water) was so difficult to be obtained. We asked them why they did not break up their settlement and go elsewhere; but this idea seemed to never to have occurred to them. They said that their fathers had lived here before them...and the right of soil is their own by inheritance. They considered most importantly, that they were better off than in the villages, where people are subject to certain municipal regulations and duties, or than (working) on the haciendas, where they would be under the control of other men."

This writing of almost two centuries ago was about a cluster of homes near the two communities we had observed. The culture of not wanting legal responsibility and the ramifications that go with it, is still existing in rural Mexico. It exists in other countries as well.

Like many other writers, I have made a few unsuccessful forays into different subject material. One such title to do with Mexico, was *Hold A Gun Or Hold A Door.* My story line had to do with the youth from this type of rural Mexico. The proposition was that there were at least six subcultures of industry and commerce, none of which are totally linked - as the young protagonists attempt to find reality in a drug war that is in effect an unspoken, all encompassing civil war.

The new Mexico, that of robotics, skilled technocrats and secured chartered banks clashes with the charlatans that present their peers as cottage industry hand baggage makers and even pimps. Billions of investment pesos pertaining to natural resources and investment dollars collide by not providing education, as these young individuals are kept in their place within a local third world country evolution.

They are ripe for recruitment as *soldiers,* by the drug cartel. International tourism, global commerce and big business agriculture seems to not be linked. That is, *they* would have menial jobs (such as a doorman) or they would be tempted to join in a life of crime. In the story-line there are the good guys and the bad guys and the choice of which group to join. Half-truths seem to dominate all the minor details.

Mexico may be at a crossroads. Should Mexico lose the drug wars, it will recede back into being a desert with a central walled and secured industrial oasis as protection. Nowhere else is a revolution so silent and nowhere else is a civil war so unrelenting but unknown outside of its border.

The premise being that in these poor communities, education is not an option and by having anti-establishment (*non) values* they could be enticed into criminal thought patterns. A caste system is perpetuated.

However, the very poor of rural Mexico now have access to relevant education through living in residence in high school, coupled with the same possibility in technical institutions. In that one fact, the premise of someone logically resorting to crime in order to succeed - is entirely invalid. Thankfully my specific book will never be written, as it is simply too redundant.

On this particular drive, on a winding road in the countryside, I was excited about viewing these groups of homes, just as they are, unpretentious. They were definitely homes, not just houses.

***

This southern trip, across Highway 186, west to east, is obviously not viewed as worthwhile to a typical tourist of Maya culture - as the number of visitors was sparse. However, the drive from Merida to the small town of Xpujil is only a little over six hours. The drive back by Highway 293 going by Chetumal, is seven hours to Merida. We very much enjoyed it and I recommend it.

***

TWENTIETH WEEK:

Being awakened by songbirds in this part of Mexico is a treat. Our beach house has two *Blue-black Split-tailed Birds* (Great Tailed Grackles) that inhabit our coconut trees. One drinks water from our swimming pool every day. The significance of this bird is its seven or eight divergent sounds - all unrelated. This bird seems to be just showing off and they are all truly one - or eight - of my favorite sounds.

The two *Blue-black Split-tailed Birds* had two offspring. Need I say that they were blueish black and looked just like them? The two chicks followed their mother around our beach yard like a small parade, enjoying the occasional insect. Twice we watched as the mother attempted to teach a smaller bird to sing like her. They would sit side-by-side on a branch (in front of us) and the chick would imitate the mother with one of the six sounds. The cuteness of it was when the chick could not get it right. We watched as over a period of time, a third, if not a fourth sound was achieved. We can only conclude that all went well and the chicks became fluent in their bird call language.

Unfortunately when they visit us, they dominate and other birds don't visit. My infatuation with them finally came to an end. One of the other incredible song birds was treating us to a song, as we enjoyed our second cup of coffee. Right in front of us, a Great Tailed Grackle swooped in and attacked the helpless little creature as it fled. The jaw-like beak of the Grackle was like scissor snips, rapidly snapping at the small bird's tail. It was the fiercest attack that I've ever seen. The songbird made it out of the area and I learned yet another lesson about nature.

* * *

A number of books relating to Mexico, refer to *Mexican Time*, an expression to the negative. The concept is that doing things tomorrow (*manana*) is good enough. I probably learned or concocted a new expression, that of *Mexican Vision*.

For the total of three years that I have lived in Mexico, like most northerners I was aware of the garbage - both along the roads and on vacant lots. Having viewed a few homes for sale, it was apparent that even a beautiful home was likely to have what appeared to be a garbage dump next door or down the street.

In Uaymitun we have a usual dumping place just across the street. It may be that this practice evolved for two reasons. Garbage of the past decades was disposable organic substances and not plastic, and the dense tropical foliage hid the substance until it deteriorated or could be burnt. Now, of course, plastic lasts forever. In actual fact I'm getting used to it and I just focus on the property or home that I am viewing or visiting. The view from the side of the property becomes irrelevant. I might just as well give that a positive name: *Mexican Vision*.

We have also developed an expression of saying, "It's possibly *Mahi-mahi*". A number of years ago, I had ordered mahi-mahi from the menu of a rather expensive restaurant in Puerto Vallarta. My reason was specific in that I wanted to compare the mahi-mahi (fish) that I had enjoyed in Hawaii. However, it seemed to taste like tuna.

When I questioned the waiter, he stated, "No of course not. We don't have mahi-mahi in Mexico."

I questioned why tuna was on the menu as mahi-mahi.

He self-righteously stated, "Because it is our equivalent."

I smiled politely, as it was a lesson learned.

Two years ago, Martha and I were dining in Ajijic, Mexico. Lake Chapala has local fish there, which were offered on the menu, simply as *fish*. Having related my frustration in my former attempt to order mahi-mahi to Martha, we were surprised at the boldness of a conversation taking place at the next table.

"What kind of fish is it?" The question was reasonable.

"*Mahi-mahi*," stated the waitress without hesitation.

Martha broke-up with laughter. Possibly she roared with laughter, I'm not sure. I was embarrassed in any case. Fortunately the group behind us just thought we were otherwise occupied.

I concluded that often in Mexico things that are not quite what they should be, are not lies, nor are they misrepresentations. When we see, for example, *Playa Chaca Beach Condo*s being advertised *as life on the beach*, when it is two blocks from the beach, or a magnificent resort advertised as if built and ready to move into, but it's only in foundation stage, we simply state that i*t's possibly Mahi-mah*i. Or if something is missing the fine print explanation - *it's possibly Mahi-mahi*.

I only have two recommendations for those who want to live in Mexico. The more *Mexican Vision* you have and the more you allow a bit of *Mahi-mahi* to happen, the happier you will be. Coping with *Mexican Time* is another issue, but it has improved over the years.

* * *

In summary, we consider five months living on the beach on the Gulf of Mexico something that we will never forget, with most of the experience of living here to be positive. The modern day Maya are possibly the most gracious, polite and friendly people in the world. We have never had a fear of anything here in Yucatan State, as in much of the rest of the world.

In walking down the Malecon in Progreso it is easy to imagine the buildings that front it in another era only twenty-some years ago. They must have been beautiful and they certainly are unique. It took me the five months to (possibly) understand what had happened to this coast. Easily one half of what were magnificent restaurants in Progreso are closed down. The same is true of the adjoining community of Chicxulub, where a former fairly large night club area is now non-functional. The buildings are entirely deserted. Near Uaymitun, further along the beach, we have small resorts that are vacant. Finally, possibly with the aid of our extensive traveling in the Yucatan Peninsula, it seems clearer.

What happened? The Maya Riviera happened! The beaches of the Gulf of Mexico were no match for the beauty and the ambiance of the Caribbean. Cancun to Tulum was developed purposely by Mexican developers to be in competition with Acapulco. In doing a great job of it, Yucatan State's beaches were blown *out of the water*.

We are among many who would enjoy an apartment condo on the Maya Riviera instead of a single family beach home here. Like many new arrivals to life in Mexico, we of course do have choices.

We wanted to learn about living long-term in a single family house, in the tropics and on the ocean. We did, as we experienced uncomfortably high winds, rusted tools and appliances within days of purchase and an overabundance of insects relative to *our* lagoon. We endured the ongoing smell of *turtle grass* washed ashore on an otherwise beautiful beach.

In the case of Uaymitun and the adjoining areas, there is a large residential vacancy rate. This meant that we didn't have a community of expats to join for any type of occasion. Nothing else seemed to be happening now this side of Merida. At first we erroneously worried about even finding a rental in one of these picturesque homes. It seems now like one out of five homes were occupied for Easter Break. That's up from the one out twenty in the weeks following.

The last week of April was interesting in that everyone *went home*. The Easter or Spring Break was over and also the *snow birds* had left. We often take walks on the beach and usually then observe our neighbors. They are now all gone. Apparently they return in June and July, only to leave before the storm season of September and October.

But it still was a wonderful five months and we are glad that we had the experience. Our next winters though will be in another part of Mexico - perhaps Puerto Escondido or back at Ajijic on Lake Chapala. We love Mexico for retirement or semi-retirement living. We actually loved it here for the five months.

TWENTY FIRST WEEK:

We calculated that our total cost for the five months, including our side trips and rental car - was less in cost than two weeks, on a luxury cruise ship liner, in the Caribbean. That isn't very adventuresome to calculate, but for most of us, it's relevant.

Returning to Vancouver in Canada from the beach was not hard at the start of May as it had warmed up there. Western Canada had just experienced the coldest winter on record. We had smiled many times as we consistently checked out the temperatures in our home country. We prefer the warm climates of Mexico.

* * *

IDEAL TOUR ROUTES:

ROUTE 1 - TWO TO THREE DAYS

The Puuc Route provides the most incredible presentation of Maya architecture. The sites are a one hour drive from each other, with the possibility of enjoying them as a group.

- Labna
- Xlapac
- Sayil
- Kabah
- Uxmal

The cave of Grutas de Loltun can easily be included if visiting for three days. If visiting from Campeche, Edzna is also perfect as an add on.

The idea that this area is the jungle of Mexico is false. In actual fact it is just *bush*. The qualification of an area to be jungle has to do with the dense undergrowth and the *jungle canopy*. The advertised idea that the tours of this route go through wilderness is a bit of *Mahi-mahi*. It is farmland with unbroken terrain - but it is the route of *perfect* ancient architecture and design!

***

ROUTE 2 - ONE DAY

Should visiting be from the Maya Riviera, then Ek Balam can be a single tour and very enjoyable. The cave of Gruta Balankanche is logically added on, making this an exciting one day trip. Many tours go to Tulum and Coba in lieu of *Route* 2, but my bias is with the authenticity of the one day's exploration. It would be an unforgettable day!

- Ek Balam
- Gruta Balankanche

*　*　*

ROUTE 3 - FOUR TO FIVE DAYS

The Rio Bec Route as a group is not a presentation of the most dynamic in Maya architecture. It is however, a group of ruined cities that will enthrall all those wanting to view the world of *lost civilizations* in their original setting. Only Calakmul provides an actual jungle wilderness and even then it is not the jungle of *Central American Rain Forests*. The drive to Calakmul needs to be challenged first thing in the morning, with the day set aside for this large site. Others may be experienced together as a challenging small group.

- Calakmul
- Balamku
- Chicanna
- Xpujil
- Becan
- Dzibanche
- Kinichna

* * *

ROUTE 4 - FOUR TO FIVE DAYS

If staying in Merida the dynamics of which ruins to give priority to will change. I have listed the ruins of the Puuc route after the two sites easily accessible from Merida.

- Mayapan
- Dzibilchaltun
- Uxmal
- Labna
- Xlapac
- Sayil
- Kabah

The cave of Grutas de Loltun can be included; the days will be long - but exciting.

***

RECOMMENDED HOTELS:

We found our hotels on Expedia and they were adequately discounted to be affordable. After staying a few nights, we considered that we had made lucky choices. They were all three star (plus) hotels and they all had a web site.

Campeche:
The is a classic colonial structure and quite sophisticated and beautiful as such. Being in the well lit city centre we were able to partake in late night drinks and dining.

Hotel Plaza Colonial
Calle 10 San Francisco de Campeche
No. 15 Col. Centro
Campeche, México

Valladolid:
The hotel is on the outskirts of town, which may make it less than ideal, but the city is not large. The hotel is quite new and contemporary. In contrast to the name, the internet connections were less than desirable.

Technotel Valladolid, Valladolid
Call 12 No.188B entre 37 y 39
Valladolid, Mexico

Playa del Carmen:
The location just off 5th Avenue was ideal for partaking in the city's downtown activities. It does have construction around it and the other older buildings close by require that you use *Mexican Vision*. The hotel is recently built and contemporary. It was Spartan in design.

Hotel 52, Playa del Carmen
Calle 52, entre 5a y 10a
Playa del Carmen, Mexico

Uxmal:
This hotel overlooks the ruins. Having walked the distance to the ruined city, I can state that it is 1.5 kilometres to the edge of the property owned by the government. The hotel infers that it is 1.5 kilometres to the gate of the ruins, which by its nature is a bit of Mahi-mahi. It is a 3 kilometre walk in the hot sun to the gate. The hotel restaurant is very good, only slightly expensive, but recommended. The ambiance of the hotel being near the Puuc Route is worth an extra day's stay, which can give time for a Chocolate Museum visit thrown it. There isn't a present day town of Uxmal.

Uxmal Resort Maya
Carretera Mérida-Campeche, Uxmal, Mexico

Xpujil:

Again we made a lucky choice. It seemed that all of the other hotels in the area were on the main highway - beside noisy traffic speeding through the small town of Xpujil. We were past the outskirts and on a side road. The hotel was designed to show off nature and it did a wonderful job of it. The exteriors of the rooms (as fourplexes) seemed almost too rustic, giving us a bit of apprehension before viewing, but the interiors were surprisingly clean, modern and spacious. The restaurant of the hotel presented delicious meals, not a lot of choice, but nevertheless exceptional. It was great fun being at this hotel *in the bush* (jungle if you prefer).

Chicanna EcoVillage Resort, Xpujil
Carretera Escarcega-Chetumal,
Xpujil, Mexico

* * *

ENJOYABLE EBOOKS ON MAYA CULTURE AND THE YUCATAN PENINSULA:

The Mayas, the Sources of Their History (and) *Dr. Le Plongeon in Yucatan, His Account of Discoveries* - by Stephen Salisbury, Jr. These two writings are from the *Proceedings of the American Antiquarian Society* of 1876 and 1877, found together as one eBook on Amazon.

History of the Spanish Conquest of Yucatan and of the Itzas (and) *Papers of the Peabody Museum of American Archaeology and Ethnology*, Harvard University - published by Philip Means as a graduate student at Harvard, in 1917 - available together as one eBook on Amazon.

Yohlik"nal of Palenque - by Leonide Martin, published in 2016 as eBook number one in a series of three. It is fiction with fantasies of characters, cities, politics and even deities. Ms. Martin is a retired professor and Maya researcher - and as such was able to write her knowledge into these chronicles, while telling the stories of the powerful women of the ancient past. I found the detail of the book almost too demanding. However it was her detail that enabled me to imagine the past of Maya beliefs and traditions - whether it be communication with the gods, the bloody sacrifices made, the hierarchal society, the feathers worn, or even the daily diet.

The Search For The Silver City. A Tale of Adventure In Yucatan - by James Otis, published in 1893. This short novel is *wonderfully* inaccurate and is pure fantasy. I enjoyed this read due to knowing that this is what much of the world incorrectly thought of the Yucatan Peninsula and the Maya, over one-hundred years ago.

* * *

My short list includes only eBooks. Maya and Mesoamerican Archaeology books in hard-copy are available throughout the world. Most are very well researched text.

Books by John Lloyd Stephens, along with the illustrations by Frederick Catherwood, initially published in the eighteen hundreds, are probably read and viewed by many of us with an interest in Maya Civilization. I especially enjoyed the 2013 Dante publication, a condensed version of *Incidents of Travel In Yucatan* by John Lloyd Stephens. It not only presents what was then his brazen disregard for, and lack of understanding, of archaeological principles, it also gives us knowledge of his accomplishment in bringing an awareness of this *lost civilization* to the rest of the world. Frederick Catherwood's drawings are priceless in that regard and also may be found under separate titles.

Archaeologists such as Sylvanus G. Morely were responsible for the creation of major field projects, which led to numerous writings in the early twentieth century.

For an indepth study, *Mayan Hieroglyphic Writing: An Introduction* and *A Catalog of Mayan Hieroglyphs*, by J. Eric S. Thompson has never been surpassed.

Tatiana Proskouriakoff illustrated Mayan glyphs and in 1960 provided a most important discovery establishing that the glyphs told of history. Throughout her work and others such as Yuri Knorozov - the idea that Mayan hieroglyphic writing is a mixed script of signs that are syllabic, while many others are logograms, was accepted. The former perception that the Maya were among the world's most gentle people is now dispelled. It had become clear that blood sacrifices were almost a daily routine in Maya rituals.

The research of the last twenty years has changed perceptions of Ancient Maya Civilization and the newer published books will reflect that change. The photographs in all of the newer books on Maya and Mesoamerican Archaeology are incredible quality. I highly recommend them.

* * *

THE 22 MAYA RUINS ALPHABETICALLY

	page
Ake	35
Balamku	107
Becan	121
Calakmul	110
Chicanna	117
Chichen Itza	55
Coba	78
Dzibanche	123
Dzibilchaltun	22
Edzna	42
Ek Balam	52
Kabah	96
Kinichna	125
Labna	91
Mayapan	19
Oxkintok	31
Sayil	94
Tulum	75
Uxmal	98
Xkambo (X'Cambo)	21
Xlapac	93
Xpujil	119

***

Thank you for reading my book.

A link to my web pages presenting my other books and eBooks is

http://LonPelletier.com

LONNIE PELLETIER ART & WRITING

125 of my paintings (as the *art of outer space*) are also shown as slide shows at my web site.

www.ingramcontent.com/pod-product-compliance
Lightning Source LLC
Chambersburg PA
CBHW041625220426
43663CB00001B/14